CRICUT

This Book Includes:
Cricut Maker & Project Ideas For Beginners. The Ultimate Guide for Beginners To Master Your Cricut Maker And The Best Projects Ideas Illustrated.

Emily Maker

TABLE OF CONTENTS

CRICUT MAKER FOR BEGINNERS

TABLE OF CONTENTS

CRICUT PROJECT IDEAS FOR BEGINNERS

CRICUT MAKER FOR BEGINNERS

The Ultimate Beginners Guide to Master Your Cricut Maker, Design Space and useful step-by-step processes for your crafts while you are at home

Emily Maker

Introduction

Like many machines that are being placed on the shelves, this device also does come with its unique software filled with different settings and features to toggle with. All these components ensure that you are using this instrument is ending up with a beautiful, customized, and accurate product. Cricut's very own software is called "Cricut Design Space," and all of Cricut's devices come with this software, whether it is Cricut mini or Cricut Explore Air. Every Cricut owner must have this software installed in their device and ready to use at any moment. The Cricut must be directly connected to the device via cable or by Bluetooth. Either way, the device needs to be close to the machine.

The software is free and has a good user interface that makes it clear and easy to work with, even if you don't have any prior experience with working with a similar device. Its user-friendly feature encourages creativity in an individual. The program is based on Cloud, so even if your device is destroyed or has become inaccessible for any reason, the different design files can be safely recovered. It can be opened onto almost every device and available at any moment. A laptop, tablet or mobile can be used as well, and starting a project on one device and switching in between to another is possible. It can even be accessed offline. After the program has been installed, you need to create the designs from the beginning or use any one of thousands of templates already stored in its library. Design Space has a large, diverse collection to push a freshman to start constructing and inventing. One can play around with varieties of fonts and images and new inspiring ideas. For optimum usage, a Cricut Explorer connected to a computer will be sufficient. This way, all of the features are available, and the machine works without lag.

What Can I Do With It?

Crafting is a hobby that knows no borders, pretty much any shape or design is achieved through this marvelous machine opening to endless uses. Any material needed to be cut engraved or etched; this machine will fulfill that need. The only boundary would be the lack of one's imagination or capability. From making a few mundane everyday accessories to creating parts of cars, this piece of technology will do the job without fault. Some ideas to use it are as follows:

- For a beginner, it is recommended that they should start working on less complicated projects such as paper crafting. Many people have made a scrapbook in High School, which may or may not be up to the mark, but with this new machine, you can create any papercraft project not only easily but also competently.

- You can use it to make paper pennants to use in a party or to use it as an accessory to bring to local games and show your support to your team. You can design and shape the flag themselves to give it a hint of uniqueness.

- Cricut can also be used to make greeting cards. Sending your loved ones a unique and customized card will not only separate you from the crowd but show them that they are special to you. Making greeting cards is very easy even for a beginner by using Cricut

- The design and uses are not only limited to paper, but you can also make a leather bracelet by using different features in the software provided. Even thick materials and complicated structures cannot hold the Cricut machine back.

- You can make iron-on Vinyl t-shirts. Customize T-shirts are usually expensive to order, but you can make it through Cricut easily.

- It can also be used to make new utensils such as customize jars, mugs, plates, etc. You can even make a doormat using this device.

- It can also be used to make home decorations. On holidays you can simply sit at home rather than go out shopping for different decorating items.

- You can make your customized pillows blankets and bedsheets

- It can also be used for making models of things such as an airplane.

- You can even design beautiful and artful pieces of jewelry.

- Some people use it to make different parts for their cars motorcycles etc. if they can't find the right parts anywhere else.

- It can also be used to make banners and signs to attract customers

What Is Cricut Access?

Cricut Access is a membership that allows the Cricut user to access thousands and thousands of different ready to use images and fonts, which are always new and fresh. With these many choices, inspiration will hit you with many great ideas and fulfill your every need. Thanks to the membership, on every purchase, there is up to 10% off on every item related to Cricut. Not only that, but the membership also provides different discounts and offers on various Cricut purchases. On Cricut Design Space, some ready to make projects will be available to use. If you want, then you can use these designs to sell and make a profit. You can even open a business from the help of the device so buying a membership will be worth it in such a scenario. Cricut access helps the Cricut users in doing what they want to do by providing them with the best deals and giving them new ideas. A new user should first learn to use the machine and then considered buying the membership. A regular user would purchase Cricut Access as it will benefit them immensely.

What Materials Can I Cut?

The biggest advantage of having a Cricut, apart from its accuracy, is being able to use a large number of versatile materials to make refined, beautiful objects. With over 100 materials that this machine can work with, you can easily maneuver around with great choices that he or she has. Whatever material that you want to work with, he or she can make full use of that material, regardless of the complexity of the structure they want to design or create. A majority thinks that this device is only used for cutting paper or some types of vinyl. Such perception may have arisen from the fact that most people using it do not fully understand its capability and lacks the skills to use the device up to its full potential. Even hard and tough material such as leather or metal, do not limit its functions. The Cricut Explore and Cricut maker can work with any material if its 2-2.4 mm thick or even less. If anyone wants to make something, chances are, his or her Cricut can make it without hindrance to the user. Some examples of the materials manipulated are listed below:

- Cricut is renowned for and can swiftly design on different kinds of paper and cardstocks. There is a great number of types of paper which are used for different reasons all across the board. Some are cardstock, construction paper, glitter paper, kraft paper, freezer paper, flocked paper, poster board, shimmer paper, wax paper, metallic paper, bond paper, gloss coated paper, matt coated paper, etc.

- The next major material use to cut by Cricut is Vinyl. It has a lot of uses, from making signs to decorations. Different types of vinyl used are Glitter vinyl, Glossy vinyl, Dry Erase vinyl, metallic vinyl, stencil vinyl, matte vinyl, etc.

- As previously stated, Cricut is not only used for cutting but also in engraving and etching. Iron on or heat transfer vinyl can be used to decorate any item in a person's possession like bags or shirts. Types of iron-on that can be used are Glossy Iron-on, Glitter Iron-on, Metallic Iron-on, Matte Iron-on, etc.

- Clothing items can be fashioned to one's desires. Any type of fabric can be shaped and embroidered. The materials range from a big list from Cotton Fabric, Leather, Metallic Leather, Linen, Flannel, Denim, Silk, Wool felt, Polyester, etc. Cricut makers can cut through Cashmere, Velvet, chiffon, jersey, and many more types of fabrics.

- Different materials like Foams, Magnet Sheets, Metallic Vellums, different plastics, and wood can be cut.

What Cricut Accessories Do I Need?

After buying the Cricut machine, the box will include with the machine a sharp blade, a cutting mat, and power cords, but the accessories required depends on the scale of the project and what kind of sophisticated design you are trying to achieve. For basic uses and cutting up papers, cardstocks, and vinyl, this setup is enough, but if you want to try an ambitious task and use somewhat different materials, Cricut accessories come in to play to help you towards your goals. The materials required are:

Cutting mats: For general use, the device comes with a light grip mat, which is a basic mat but has its limitations. There are more types of mats. The StandardGrip mat is mainly used for vinyl and iron-on. If you want to use heavier materials or glossy materials, then they should use a strong grip mat. It will provide enough friction that the material will not slide off the mat, and the cutting process will be smooth. For textile and fabric cutting, a fabric grip mat can be used, which is exclusive for the use of clothing items.

Blades: When you purchase the machine, the blade that comes with it, a Fine Point Blade, will be enough for more than the general use of the device. There are, however, two more blades to choose from in a Cricut Explorer. The first blade is called the Deep Point Blade which is used for cutting harder objects such as magnetic sheets, cardboard, and thicker card stocks. The second one is called Fabric Bonded Blade, which is the same blade as the Fine Pointed one. It only matches the fabric grip mat, and it is used separately for fabrics so that both blades last for a long period. If the cuts on materials by the machine are not as crispy or smooth, a replacement FinePoint Blade can be bought.

Pens: they are not a necessity, but if someone does a lot of paper crafting or generally has bad handwriting, these pens will help them make prettier and more beautiful designs.

Other required accessories are

- tweezers (For finely replacing some parts)

- Scissors

- Spatula to lift the cut pieces

- Weeder to weed out extra pieces

- Scrapper or an XL scraper for cleaning.

- Scoring stylus and scoring blade

Other accessories for a serious user includes:

- Cricut Easy Press which makes working with Iron-on very easy

- Cricut bright pad, which protects the eye when designing using the software

- Full Cricut toolset and mat set with different varieties of instruments

Chapter 1 What is Cricut Machine and How To use it?

The Cricut Machine is a cutting machine also known as craft plotter or Cricut Explore Air. It functions like a regular printer, but it has some differences as compared to how a regular printer functions.

Cricut Machine has a small blade scaled inside the machine, and it can cut material up to 12" in width. When the material is ready to cut, it is placed on the mat and is sent into the machine. The blade present inside the machine moves on the material and cuts it according to the given directions with the use of a series of rollers as well. After the material is cut, the mat is unloaded, and the material is then peeled off from it. It helps you build your own creativity by providing you enough room to think of a design and then give it life.

People who are into crafts and do-it-yourself designs all around the world are very familiar with Cricut and their innovative cutting machines. Cricut is the most popular brand name for die-cutting machines, also called cutting plotters or craft plotter machines. It can be used for simple projects like scrapbooking or very elaborate projects like making Christmas decorations.

A Cricut machine can be likened to a printer, especially because of the design. But, the Cricut machine won't print out your design. Instead, it will cut the design out from the material you're using! So, you can make a design on your computer, and the machine will cut it out of fabric, paper, cardboard, vinyl, and even the most unlikely materials. When using some Cricut models, you can print out your design on whatever material of your choosing.

Hence it provides the user the satisfaction that how the end design would look like.

This machine is used for several purposes such as card makers and also by scrapbookers. Different options such as portrait mode or landscape mode can be added as well. One of another feature of this machine is that different kind of blades and mats can be used depending upon the design we want as an output. We can alternatively change different blades, markers, and mats to get the image, design, and product of our choice. Hence, this machine really helps in building your own creativity and bringing to life by using various techniques.

The cricut maker machine is an electronic die-cutter for different materials including papers, vinyl and fabrics into desired shapes and patterns. This machine is capable of awesome design cuts and markings on a large variety of materials and very easy to use.

The cricut machines have the capability to cut large number of materials accurately and quickly. The range of materials varies from the delicate paper to leather then to thicker materials such as wood. With the aid of powerful rotary blades, the machine glides and rolls over any fabrics effortlessly leaving smooth and accurate cut on the material.

In addition to this awesomeness, a digital sewing pattern library is stored in the cricut maker for the user to access hundreds of patterns from different brand names such as Riley Blake and Simplicity. You can pick a number of projects from the library and boom, the machine cuts every piece you desire.

The Cricut Design Space allows the user to access any one of the over 50 projects in its library including 25 digital sewing patterns. Not only that, it also allows you to upload an image to create a customized design of your own. The capabilities of the Cricut Maker Machine are just endless: Iron-on decorations on t-shirts, leather, vinyl decors, wood puzzles and sewing projects are some of the DIY or craft projects you can do using the machine.

The Cricut can be used for plenty of different designs so long as your creativity permits. All you need is an idea, your creativity, a space for your craft, your material to cut as, well as your trusty Cricut machine.

There are plenty of crafts that you can create with your Cricut—it makes crafting easier, simpler and faster using this machine. If you are new to using the Cricut, fret not. You will be given the basics of the machine and how to use it appropriately. You will also be introduced to common, everyday crafts for beginners to give you a good understanding of the Cricut Machine. Doing common crafts will help you understand your machine and potentially lead you to explore what other things you can do with it.

The generic title for the Cricut is a die cutter, craft plotter, or a smart cutting machine. The format of this machine allows you to create projects from flat materials of varying thicknesses. The projects that you can do with this tool can range from simple to quite complex, depending on your skill level with these materials. Depending on the sharpness of the blade in your cutting machine, or the model that you're using, your materials can range anywhere from craft felt to thin sheets of metal. This gives you an idea of how vast the range really is, for what this machine can help you to accomplish as a crafter.

Other machines of this type can run you several hundred or even thousands of dollars, require design degrees, come with complex proprietary software, and offer only a fraction of the design options that come with Cricut, and the proprietary, user-friendly Cricut Design Space. Cricut's massive base of users are always sharing the latest and greatest in projects, tips, tricks, guides, and new materials to use with your Cricut machine. As a crafter with a Cricut machine, your resources are nearly limitless.

In one organized place, you'll be able to access all the information you need on how to use the software, project guides that take you from start to finish, a list of all that you will need, and so much more. This is your comprehensive guide that you can refer to again and again, no matter how your skill level grows over time!

I'm intent on bringing you all the most important knowledge on the subject of Cricut, what it can do, how to get the most out of your machine, and how to consistently get the best results.

Types of cricuts

Cricut Explore One

In terms of what is currently available from Cricut, this is the most basic machine they offer. This machine boasts being able to cut 100 of the most popular materials that are currently available to use with your Cricut machine, as well as being perfectly user friendly

The Cricut Explore One is considered to be the no-frills beginner model of Cricut craft plotters and operates at a lower speed than the other models available. Unlike the others available in the current product line, the Cricut Explore One has only one accessory clamp inside, so cutting or scoring, and drawing cannot be done simultaneously. They can, however, be done in rapid succession, one right after the other.

While this is a great tool for a wide range of crafts on 100 different materials, and which can get you well on your way to designing breathtaking crafts that are always a cut above others, the cost is not as high as you might imagine. If you intend to use your craft plotter mainly for those special occasions where something handcrafted would be perfect, then this a great machine to have on hand.

Cricut Explore Air

This model does have two on-board accessory clamps, which allow for simultaneous marking and cutting or scoring. These clamps are marked with an A and a B so you can be sure your tools are going in the right places,

every time you load them in.

This model is equipped to handle the same 100 materials as the Cricut Explore One, and operates at the same speed, so the price difference reflects those differences and the similarities! This is a great value for the powerhouse that you're getting.

Cricut Explore Air 2

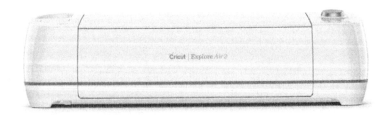

It is the current top selling craft plotter and is arguably the best value they have to offer for the price. This model cuts materials at twice the speed of the previous two models, has Bluetooth capability, and has the two on-board accessory clamps.

For someone who finds themselves using their Cricut with any regularity, this is the best machine for the job. You will be able to do your crafts twice as fast, and you will get a satisfactory result every time, even at that speed!

Cricut Maker

The Cricut Maker is considered to be Cricut's flagship model. This is the one that can do just about anything under the sun on just about any material you can fit into the mat guides of your machine. The one drawback of this powerhouse model is the price point.

This does make this model more prohibitive, unless you plan to make crafts that you can sell with this model. If this is your intention, you can rest assured that whatever you turn out with this machine will be the best of the best, every single time. If you're selling your crafts, this baby will pay for itself in little to no time at all.

For the avid crafter who likes to show up to the party with the most gorgeous crafts that are leaps and bounds ahead of their peers, this machine might be overkill for the price. Of course, if you are keeping up with the Joneses, this is the model to have.

This model really does have it all and we can prove it. No other Cricut machine has the speed that the Cricut Maker has. The cuts that can be made with the special precision blades that fit only this machine, are crisper than anything you could ever hope for from a straight knife or other craft cutter. The blade housings allow you to simply remove the tip from the housing, install the next one, clip it back into place, and keep on rolling through your projects. In addition to this, the machine can detect the material loaded into it, so you won't need to set the type of materials at the beginning of each of your projects.

Chapter 2 What Tools and Accessories Can You Use with a Cricut Machine?

I t's hard to think that anyone who buys a Cricut Machine will get a full-option one, as the standard machine will not cover all your cutting needs. However, Cricut will give you the option to improve your cutting machine by using some of its available tools like pens, weeding tools, tool kits, precision cutting tools, rulers, self-healing mats, and of course, blades.

When it comes to pens, Cricut can provide you its very own labeled products that are compatible with these machines. It allows you to draw and create your project without having to think about Design Space. If you are very gifted at drawing, and you want to give a more personal touch to the project you are working on, then you definitely need to try Cricut pens. Some users find the Cricut Pens kind of expensive, and they just purchase regular pens with an adapter to use them directly on Cricut. As you can imagine, the manufacturer encourages the use of Cricut products for better results.

If you truly want to become a pro at cutting with these machines, then it's highly recommended to go for any precision cutting tool (like the TrueControl Kit), as they normally include a knife, a ruler, and a self-healing mat. As you probably know, a normal cutting mat will last between 25 and 40 cuts, but this mat is not for use inside the Cricut Machine. It simply prevents blade cut-through, making it the right foundation for any precision cutting project.

Now, these are the tools you can use with a Cricut Machine to enhance your performance, so if you really want to become better and create more diverse projects, then you really need to spend some money on purchasing the tools mentioned above. Since Cricut is making you transform your passion into a business, you always have to learn more and be prepared to try new tools on these machines, otherwise, you will not be able to stay ahead of the game.

Obviously, the Cricut Machine doesn't come fully equipped with all possible blades. Depending on the material you are planning to cut, there are several types of blades you will need to consider. Over time, the manufacturer has created 10 types of blades, but the flagship machine (Cricut Maker) is only compatible with six of them. Therefore, Cricut has the Premium Fine Point Blade and Housing, the Deep Point Blade and Housing, the Bonded Fabric Blade and Housing (these blades are compatible with the Cricut Maker machine and whole Cricut Explore Family), the Rotary Blade and Housing, the Knife Blade and Housing, but also the Scoring Wheel (or Double Scoring Wheel) and Housing. All the blades mentioned above are compatible with Cricut Maker.

Other blades like the Standard Blade Housing and Fine Point Blades, the Deep Cut Blade and Housing, the Scoring Tip and Housing, or the Cricut Cake Blade and Housing, are compatible with older models of

Cricut Machines like the Cricut Personal, Cricut Create, Cricut Expression, Cricut Expression 2, Cricut Imagine, Cricut Cake and Cricut Cake Mini.

It's important to understand what each blade can be used for if you want to purchase them as accessories in the near future. So let's go through each of these blades to find out more about them.

Premium Fine-Point Blade

This type of blade can be used to cut a wide variety of materials, from thin to medium-weight ones, and it's specialized in making very complicated cuts. You probably heard of it as the Premium German Carbide Blade, and it can be found in all Explore family machines.

Good to know:

- this blade is highly recommended for cardstock, paper, poster-board, iron-on, vinyl, but other thin to medium weight materials as well

- you can find this blade in two colors: silver or gold

- it can be used with its own housing, or with the Bonded Fabric blade housing

Deep Point Blade

Just like the previous blade, this one can also be included in the fine point blades category. This blade can help you perform more complicated cuts on an even wider variety of materials. The blade angle is steeper (60 degrees compared to 45 degrees for other fine point blades), and the steel used is harder and more durable.

Bonded-Fabric Blade

If you want to have an accurate cut and not mess with fabric, you definitely don't want to use scissors to cut such a material. Therefore, you really need a special blade to prolong the fabric-cutting life. This is what the Bonded-Fabric Blade is for, as it can give you all the functionality of the Premium Fine-Point Blade, but it comes in pink to match the FabricGrip Mat, just for you to know which blade is designated for bonded fabrics, and which for other materials.

Good to know:

- it's highly recommended for more complicated cuts on fabrics or bonded fabrics, but it needs an iron-on backer

- it can be used with its own backer, but it also fits (and works) with the Premium Fine-Point housing

Rotary Blade

If you want to have a more customized and accurate fabric cutting, then you definitely need to use the rotary blade on your Cricut Maker. This unique blade can cut all fabrics without having a backer material.

Good to know:

- it's highly recommended to be used with soft, delicate, not very dense materials (cork or tissue paper), or with fabrics

- when using this blade, the minimum recommended image size is ¾". Smaller images can cause the blade to make a small turn (and even scrape the material). This can even lead to a gouge in your mat, and will significantly damage the life of the blade

- it can only be used with the Rotary Blade Housing

- this blade should be used with the FabricGrip mat, as this one can withstand intense pressures (it's made of more dense material)

- the housing for this blade comes with a plastic cover (just over the gear of the blade). It's highly recommended to keep this cover on to prevent any other material, or even hair, from being caught in the gears

Knife Blade

If you want to use the Cricut Maker to cut through stronger materials and up to 3/32" thick, then you really need to use the Knife Blade, as it's ideal to cut thicker materials (but in moderate detail).

Good to know:

- you can use this blade to cut chipboard, matboard, or even balsa wood (and other thicker materials)

- it can only be used with its housing

- when using this blade to cut, you may need to move to the side the star wheels on the roller bar, in order to avoid leaving tracks on your materials

Scoring Wheel and the Double Scoring Wheel

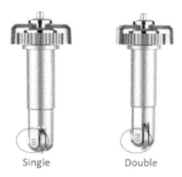

Single   Double

When you want to operate on your materials with more pressure, even 10 times more than the Scoring Stylus can handle, you really need to use one of these two blades: Scoring Wheel and the Double Scoring Wheel, if you wish to simply create crisp creases in both thick or thin materials, and to make amazing folds without any effort.

Good to know:

- The Scoring Wheel can make a deep, single scoreline, which is just perfect for light or uncoated materials, such as light cardstock, crepe paper, or even acetate

- The Double Scoring Wheel leaves two parallel and deep score lines, which are the ones you need for heavier materials like cardboard or poster board

- changing the blades is very easy and it's facilitated by the QuickSwap Housing

- there is a plastic cover placed over the gear at the top of the housing. To prevent any other material, or even hair, from getting caught in the gears, you really need to keep the plastic cover on

Fine Point Blade

This is the standard replacement blade, and is usually sold with green or grey protective caps. It's normally used on Cricut Personal, Create, Expression, Expression 2, and Imagine.

Standard Blade Housing

Replacing the housing for your blade can be something very common, so naturally, the manufacturer has created spare parts for such scenarios. The blade housing can be made of plastic or metal, and in all cases, its color is green.

Cricut Deep Cut Blade and Housing

A very good blade for cutting thicker and denser materials is the Cricut Deep Cut Blade. The housing for these blades is blue, and the protective caps are also blue. Just like other blades designed for cutting thick materials, the angle of the blade is steeper compared to normal blades (it's 60 degrees). Also, in this case, the housing is shorter to permit an open gap for thicker materials, even up to 1.5 mm thick.

You can use this blade to cut magnets, chipboards, stiffened felt, stamp materials, thick cardstock, cardboard, fabric, foam sheets, but also other thicker materials.

If you only want to create score lines, instead of cutting, then you need to consider the Cricut Scoring Tip with Housing.

For all Cricut Cake and Cake Mini users, the manufacturer still has some accessories you can use with these machines

Chapter 3 The Design Space Application

How do you make Cricut designs?

Each machine uses its own brand software, and can be downloaded and run free of charge. The Cricut Project Space software can even be used!

Project Space is very easy to use. You can create templates and upload images from scratch. You can also import cut files created by others, buy designs directly from the developer and change any of them to customize them.

Is Cricut Design Space hard to use?

No. No. So, it's so easy to use! Throughout the years I've used many different design programs and I definitely struggled with some.

The program of Cricut Design Space is as basic as it could be while still allowing you the freedom to make your designs and projects innovative.

How does Cricut Design Space Work?

What a Cricut machine is and how Cricut Design Space works is just like your project recipe. In Design Space, what you do only tells your computer where to cut, rate, or compose.

When your system is connected to your computer or another device, it can only complete a full design if only one move is taken.

Your Cricut can communicate instructions on display on your monitor or tablet screen if there are several steps. It can tell you if and when other project steps are required. For starters, you will be told to load your next sheet of paper or swap different colors of styles.

Choose A Font

Press to open the file and save it.

Tip: Set up a folder for all your fonts, and there will be no end once you start collecting!

Your Cricut font will most likely be downloaded as a zip file. You can right-click the file and click to extract everything.

Open the Cricut Font File

Find the file on your computer and open the TrueType font file (double-click). It opens up to a font view. Depending on your source, you can only obtain a TrueType file and have no other choices.

Install the Font

To install the font on your computer, click the Install button.

Cricut Font Problems

Now that the font has been mounted on your screen, it's all there! You can now scan and use the new font in Cricut Design Space.

I go into the Design Space sometimes, and after creating a text box I find my font, but it doesn't appear properly. Don't your downloaded fonts appear in Cricut?

You have to do this in order to get your font to show up in Design Space: first, try to refresh the page and see if it brings the genuine font through. If not, sign in and outside the Design Space and check to see if that does the job.

Customizing Fonts in Design Space

You can now change the font.

You may adjust the font size, style, and increase or decrease the space between letters. You can also ungroup the text in each letter to transfer each letter manually, as you like.

This makes them an image, and the design is cut like a single piece. You can do several things with Cricut & fonts: see how you can edit fonts in the Design Space to download all of the options.

How to Filter Fonts

You can search fonts by single layer cutting, multi-layer cutting and writing to find the unique font that you need. It is great to find fonts that have the option to compose. For fonts with the writing choice, the text style can also be modified to the Edit row.

You can then see what your text is like: make sure either you set or attach your letters so that the texts are drawn exactly the same way they are drawn on the canvas, otherwise the letters will be mixed together.

How To Use Weld In Cricut Design Space

Understanding how to solder in Cricut opens the door for many additional tasks. It will be a resource you use often. The welding tool can be found below the layers panel in the lower right corner of Design Space. There it is next to the slice, flattening and contour devices.

In Cricut Design Space, what does weld do? It helps you to:

• combine multiple forms and layers with a full single-layer image

• Remove cutting lines from multiple forms and cut them as a big picture

• linking script and italics so that they cut as one word and not a single letter

I have a step-for-step welding guide below.

• Instead, by clicking on a layer, by holding down' ctrl' and selecting another layer, pick the layers to weld together.

• Click ' weld' with both layers picked. When you're welding all layers on your canvas, you can pick all layers in the top bar and then press weld.

• As the joint welding of several layers transforms it into a picture, it is cut on one mat in a single color. Therefore, all your layers will become the same color once you have clicked on weld.

The weld option cannot be used until you have selected multiple layers.

How To Weld Letters With Cricut

In order to solder messages, you must first ensure that all letters are reached.

• Reduce letter distance until all letters are affected, or press' advanced' and then' ungroup to letters,' then switch letters manually.

• Once all of them touch, select and click weld.

Birthday Cake Topper Using Cricut Weld

Here's how to attach cursive Cricut letters.

• Next, I have to decrease the letter gap. The choice is at the top and right of the font size.

• If you still have some big gaps after decreasing the letter spacing, you must manually move the letters. Tap' advanced' and then' letters ungroup.' Move letters closer together to touch them all.

Both letters now strike, so I'm ready to sweat. In the layer panel you can see that if I cut it out without soldering it, it would cut out all letters instead of one word. The word must therefore be welded together. Pick everything and press solder.

It's priced together now. You can see this in the layer column, where' welding' is shown and only one image is shown. Once a term is welded together, it will cut as one-layered image exactly as it appears on the mirror. This is how the Cricut Explorer Air 2 and the Cricut Creator are cut off. For both machines, it works the same.

How To Weld Shapes With Cricut

I used the shape method here to build three circles I put into place. If I were to cut it now, three different circles (shown in the layer panel) would still be cut out. So, I have to weld it together to make a big shape. It's easy.

I've hit "pick all," then "weld"!

Now you will see that the cut lines have vanished when the circles were overlapping. There are no more three circles but one picture of one sheet. In the layer panel on the right,' welding result' is shown.

How To Edit Text In Cricut Design Space

I will follow all the different ways in which you can use Cricut to edit text, but will work with all the text icons in the Design Space Canvas.

How To Add Text In Cricut Design Space

Tap the text symbol on the left side to create a new text window. You can edit it with the box around it once you've written a text. You can:

- Remove it

- Rotate it

Unlock to change the text proportions. The height and width are always equivalent when the text is closed. Unlock to adjust the text's height or width. Increase or decrease text size by dragging it in or out.

With the icons around the lowest row, from left to right, you can:

- Adjust the font

- Style-Regular, bold, italic, bold italic or writing Style

- Changes font size

- Change the letter spacing

- Change the line spacing

- Change text lines–left, middle or right

- Flow upwards or downwards

- Advanced features

Multi-layer, single-layer or writing filter fonts. Learn how to download and install free fonts for Design Space use on your computer.

Changing the Font Style

You can change your text style to a regular, bold, italic or bold italic style.

Changing the Font Size

The font size can be changed. Type a number or press up or down the arrows to increase or reduce your text's scale.

Changing the Letter Spacing

You can adjust the text's letter spacing. To increase or decrease space between letters, click the arrows up or down.

Changing the Line Spacing

You can adjust the distance between the lines. Press up or down the arrows to increase or decrease the distance between text lines.

Changing the Text Alignment

You can change your text alignment. You can either align to the left, center or right.

Curving Text

It's possible to curve your text. Drag the button to the right or left to curve up or down your email. The further you go to the left or right, the more dramatic the curve is.

Ungrouping Text to Letters

To separate the letters in the text, click' advanced' and' ungroup to letters.' You can now move each letter individually and customize your text further.

Ungrouping Text to Lines

Select "advanced" and "file union" to control a single text thread. You can now organize several text lines exactly as you want.

Changing the Linetype

Adjust the line form to choose whether to cut or draw your Cricut text.

Changing Pen Type & Color

After you select "Draw," you can click the next box and choose the type and color of the pen. You can select your material color if you select "cut" as your linetype.

Color & Pattern Fill

If you want to print and cut your text, select line-type' cut' and fill out' print.' Select the next box to pick a color or pattern to fill in your text.

You will print this out with your printer, and then place it in your Cricut to cut the text out.

Slicing Text with Cricut

You can use the slice tool to slice text out of a form or cut one form out of another.

Put the text where you want it sliced out and then select both layers in the bottom right corner and click on the slice. Switch the layers to your hand to see the new design.

Welding Text

Use the welding feature in the Design Space to join text into one image. Instead of cutting out individual letters, the Cricut is cut as one word around the text.

To effectively use this function, the letters must all touch each other as you glue them together!

Decreasing the spacing of the letter or clicking "advanced" and "ungroup to letters" and moving all the letters manually to prevent breaking. Then pick everything and press solder.

Chapter 4 Tips and Techniques of Cricut Design Space

Cricut Design Space Tips – On the Design Canvas

1. Test your search terms. I've discovered that the search work in the Design Space Image Library can be somewhat specific. A truly conventional term that I think would yield a wide range of pictures in some cases won't. However, should I change a word or even a solitary letter, abruptly, more pictures populate. Accordingly, I suggest messing with a lot of search terms to discover precisely what you're searching for.

Here is what I mean: If I type "Dots" into the search bar, it yields around 115 pictures.

However, if I type in "dot" in the singular, it yields more than 200 pictures. When in doubt, I find that leaving off the "s" in my ventures yields significantly more results!

Another smart idea is to look through equivalent words (synonyms) because each picture is labeled with various inquiry terms. For instance, when I am hoping to cut marks, I will regularly look up label, tag, square shape, circle, and square to ensure I see all possible pictures! Similarly, I'd search bloom, plant, garden for Spring-themed pictures; and heart, love, Valentine, and so on for that theme.

2. See more from the same cartridge. When you use the search function, you may discover one picture that you love amidst an entire assortment of different pictures that you don't. What do you do when you would like to see more pictures similar to the one you like? The best place to begin is with the cartridge (set) that it originated from. To rapidly and effectively get to the cartridge, click the little data hover (I) in the bottom right-hand corner of each picture inside the Design Space Image Library (lower left). It will open up the picture details with an interactive (green) link that will take you to the full arrangement of pictures (bottom right)! That is my preferred method to discover pictures like the one I discovered using search!

3. Use free images and text. I am a huge fan of the Cricut Access membership if you are a regular crafter as I am. In any case, I understand that many individuals, particularly amateurs, might not have any desire to spend additional money to use their machines, especially at the beginning. In case you're simply learning your way around and want to mitigate your crafting costs, make sure to use the free assets of Cricut Design Space. To find these free pictures, use the filter inside the Design Space Image Library. Just check the "Free" option to see a variety of pictures you can embed into your ventures at no expense!

Your Cricut machine can also cut any font you already have on your computer. That not means that you not only can cut any font that already came on your PC, yet also, but also any typeface you can download from the Internet. Font Squirrel and DaFont are great resources. To discover the textual styles you can use without extra cost, pick "My Fonts" from the text style menu channel. That will give all of you the fonts included on your PC, plus any Cricut fonts you may have bought (either exclusively or using a Cricut Access pass). This is an extraordinary method to guarantee you are using fonts you don't need to pay for!

4. Re-color quickly. The Color Sync tool is an extraordinary way to save time on your projects and guarantee you are using similar hues across various designs. When you place a few plans onto your Design Canvas, you may wind up with different shades of the same color (e.g., 3 distinct greens, 4 unique blues, and so on). Instead of choosing each layer to re-shade it, use the Color Sync tool along with the right-hand apparatus board.

Here, you can not only view all the hues presently being used on your project, you can also relocate any layer of your design to another shading previously used. Regardless of whether you need to keep constant hues over your plans or rapidly make certain layers a specific shade for more productive cutting, this is the speediest and most straightforward approach to do it.

5. The Hide tool. When I am taking a shot at a project, I regularly pull heaps of pictures to play with. Be that as it may, when it comes time to start my activities, I need to remove everything on my canvas. Likewise, there are times when I need to cut/re-cut one piece of the

structure. Rather than erasing pictures off my canvas to prevent cutting them, I will cover them up by tapping the image of the eye by the specific picture on the right-hand Layers Panel. Any picture that is "covered up" isn't removed from your canvas, but it won't be incorporated when you send your task to be cut. The "Hide" image flips on/off, making it quite easy to cut just what you need as well as keep your canvas mess-free without losing track of pictures you may still need to play with!

6. Change any line to Cut, Score, or Draw. Quite a long time ago, if you needed a line to be drawn or scored (as opposed to cut), you needed to discover a plan with those particular qualities. Yet a recent feature of Design Space now permits ANY line to be effectively changed from cut to score to draw with the basic Linetype drop-down menu on the top toolbar.

Most plans will populate on your canvas as a "Cut" structure. However, you can without much effort change the layout of the picture to be drawn (using the pens) or scored (using the scoring apparatus or scoring wheel). Ensure your layers are un-gathered and un-appended to change how your structure will turn out.

Cricut Design Space Tips – On the Cut Screen

1. Move items around on the mat. Did you realize that you can move things around the mat on the cut screen itself? While the Design Space programming will auto-populate your pictures onto the mats

depending on their shading and direction, they may not be actually where you need them to be.

Just by relocating the pictures, you can move a cut anyplace on the mat and even pivot it using the handles on the upper right-hand corner. That not only permits you to scrunch things up more tightly than the software originally recommends, it also guarantees your cut is where you need it to be, like if you are attempting to use an irregularly shaped bit of material. Ensure you coordinate the network lines on the screen to the framework lines on your mat to guarantee that your design accommodates your material.

2. Move images starting with one mat then onto the next. Aside from moving pictures around a solitary mat, you can also move any picture starting on one mat to another, all without returning to the plain canvas and changing its shading. Then select "Move to another mat." Configuration Space will then ask you to pick which mat you'd prefer to put that particular picture on. Notice how the one-star has moved from the turquoise mat to the pink mat!

3. Save your most commonly used material settings. I'm a bit embarrassed that it took me such a long time to find this element. Back when I was using my Cricut Explore Air 2, I wouldn't use the Custom materials option since I usually had my machine set to Vinyl, Cardstock, or Iron-On. However, when I changed to the Maker, I learned I needed to use the Custom Materials menu in Cricut Design Space every single time because there is no dial to choose the material you are cutting.

I was so tired of looking through the 200+ custom material options to locate the Vinyl, Medium Cardstock, and Everyday Iron-On settings again and again. It was then that I realized you could "Top Choice" options — essentially "favorite" them. It took me all but a couple of minutes to go through the Materials menu and select the ones I used frequently. By tapping the star in the Materials menu itself, and afterward picking "Top Choices" rather than "Well Known" under Materials, you will be left with a small menu of the materials you cut most often! This is a genuine mental stability saver!

4. Skip and repeat mats. Probably the most delightful thing about how Design Space functions is that you don't need to give a lot of attention once you send your structure to cut. For whatever length of time that you use the correct shading and size paper into your machine similarly as it's appeared on the left half of your cut screen, your project should turn out as you planned it! In any case, you may find that you need to skip around which mat is cut first, re-cut a specific mat, or skip a mat all together. Fortunately, it's really simple and doesn't require exiting out of the cut screen. Before you load your mat into the machine, you can physically choose which mat will be cut next just by clicking on it on the left-hand side. The machine will then bounce to whatever mat you have selected.

You can likewise do something very similar to re-cut a specific mat, regardless of whether there is a checkmark next to the mat (which shows it has just been cut). That is a good way to cut products of a similar plan without copying it on your project canvas.

5. Connect several machines at once. I understand that most people likely don't have more than one Cricut machine. But on the off chance you do, you can connect both machines to your Design Space account simultaneously, either through Bluetooth or USB. Furthermore, don't stress over removing an incorrect plan with the wrong machine. Regardless of the number of machines you have connected, your very first step on the finished product screen is to choose which machine you need to use on the top dropdown menu. Then you can be certain that you're using the correct machine for your task!

Chapter 5 Vinyl Tricks

The Cricut Maker machine can do so much more for you and that includes making things better for you while you are crafting. If you are a beginner, you will certainly enjoy some amazing vinyl tricks like how to easily cut vinyl for decorations and clothing.

Cricut Transfer Tape

The Cricut Transfer Tape is designed to make the transfer of vinyl designs to project materials or surfaces easy. It makes it easy for you to position your design in the right place.

There are different types of transfer tape that you can use. There is the paper transfer tape, strong grip transfer tape, and regular transfer tape.

Paper transfer tape is typically made of paper. It's mostly used for curved projects. However, this transfer tape is not something you can reuse.

Strong grip transfer tape is stronger and more sticky than the paper and is used on thick vinyl.

The regular transfer tape is commonly used and is suitable for all pieces of vinyl. An example of this type of regular transfer tape is Oracle MT80P.

Using the Cricut Transfer Tape

1. Place the vinyl clear liner down into your Cricut Maker mat.

2. Select and size the image(s).

3. Load the mat into the Cricut Maker machine. Adjust the setting of your machine by selecting "Browse all materials".

4. Select the type of vinyl you are using, so that the liner is intact. This is called a kiss cut.

5. Tap the Go button.

6. Weed any piece away from your images using weeding tools that are found in the Weeding Tool Set to make the process neater and faster.

7. Take your transfer tape. Put it over the top of your project, rubbing it from one to the other till it's completely placed on the vinyl. This is to avoid any wrinkles or bubbles beneath the transfer tape. Remember to place the adhesive upside down.

8. Grab a roller to smoothen the transfer tape over the vinyl. This is to get bubbles or wrinkles out should they exist and make sure that the vinyl stays glued to the transfer tape.

9. Peel the vinyl away from the liner. This should be done at a 45-degree angle. If the vinyl refuses to come off the liner,

use your roller to rub the tape onto the vinyl till it comes off the liner.

10. Once you are done, then, it's time to put the vinyl on your project.

11. Place the vinyl over your project material in the place where you want it.

12. Grab your roller once again to rub the vinyl on the material till you are sure it's tight.

13. Carefully pull off the transfer tape.

14. You are done using your transfer tape.

Types of Vinyl to layer

There are two major types of vinyl layers.

- **The adhesive vinyl**

- **The heat transfer vinyl**

The Adhesive Vinyl

The adhesive vinyl type ranges based on thickness, brand, colors and different sizes. You can apply the adhesive vinyl on your design and then, do some weeding. After that, you apply the transfer tape. Transfer the vinyl to your design material and remove it after use.

Other brands of adhesive vinyl types include:

Oracle 631, Oracle 641, Oracle 651, Oracle 751, Oracle 951, Oracle 5600, Oracle 6510, Oracle 8300, Oracle 8510, Oracle 8710, Oramask, Oraguard, Glitter StyleTech FX, Glitter StyleTech Ultra, Siser Removable EasyPSV, StyleTech 4000, Siser Permanent EasyPSV, and so many others. Most of this adhesive vinyl has up to 2-year durability and comes in several colors.

While these adhesive pieces of vinyl are good to use, some are more suitable for outdoor use than indoor use. For example, the Glitter StyleTech FX is more suited for outdoor use.

The Heat Transfer Vinyl

Heat Transfer Vinyl or HTV as it's widely called is not a sticky vinyl like the adhesive. Instead, it makes use of heat before it could be applied to fabrics. The shiny part is placed face down, while the back of the vinyl faces upwards using the mirror technique. Once you are done with weeding, you can now paste it on your material. There is no transfer tape required because it is not sticky.

Like the adhesive vinyl, the HTV comes in a variety of colors and brands. Among them are:

Siser EasyWeed, Siser EasyWeed Electric, Siser Glow, Siser Holographic, Siser Brick 600, Siser StripFlock Pro, Siser Metal, Siser VideoFlex Glitter, and so many others.

Setting up a surface for layering

Before you try to use an adhesive, you have to make sure the surface you are using for the layering is suitable. Most pieces of vinyl work on solid surfaces like wood, plastic, and glass. There is every chance that dusts will accumulate on the surface, so apply some alcohol on it and wipe down and across the surface.

Vinyl on Wall

You can personalize your wall with some vinyl wall décor made with your Cricut Maker machine using a Cricut cartridge. That is another pretty amazing thing you can use your Cricut Maker machine for.

If you don't know the processes involved in applying it to your wall, follow these simple steps.

1. Select the perfect space for your decal or image design.

2. Clean the surface where you want to apply your decal by removing dirt and oil with a sponge and soap.

3. Place the decal on the wall. Remove the adhesive side and paste it on the selected area slowly.

4. Use a roller to remove any bubble or squeeze.

5. Remove the paper backing that is protecting the face of your decal or image design.

Iron-On Vinyl

Iron-on vinyl is a type of Vinyl material that works with the application of heat. It's a heat-sensitive material that can be used on fabrics, wood, paper, metals, etc.

There are three methods that you can use to apply iron-on vinyl on your material – a heat press, an iron, and an EasyPress are what you can use to adhere to your material.

Weeding Iron-On Vinyl

Iron-on vinyl is one of those materials that are convenient to work with on a Cricut Maker machine. It can work on difficult surfaces like wood and makes it easier to layer your projects. You can simply cut your design, weed it, and then, iron it on.

As stated here, after you just have cut your design, you have to weed it. Weeding iron-on vinyl is removing unwanted materials from your project. It's a simple process, but you need to be careful while doing it, especially if your design is a little complex.

Before you start weeding, make sure you mirror your design. Cricut will send you a warning, reminding you to do this, since you are using iron-on vinyl material. If you don't mirror your image, the weeding will turn out pretty bad because you are meant to cut the back of your vinyl. Hence, there is need to mirror the images.

Once your image has been cut, weeding is the next process. It can be indeed frustrating if you have bad eyesight, but it's pretty easy if you follow the steps below to learn how to weed your design.

1. Find a weeding hook that is convenient for you. Cricut offers a variety of weeding tools with several weeding hooks.

2. Keep your material on your Cricut mat. It's very convenient because it will keep your project steady and make it easier to weed your vinyl.

3. If you have some difficulties seeing your weeding lines, use the Cricut BrightPad. It's a small thin light of that emits light. You can place your vinyl on top of it and use the light to weed.

4. The Cricut BrightPad may not be enough, so make sure you weed under a bright light.

5. Start from the top and weed down and across. Weed slowly and carefully and ensure that nothing is removed from the back of the material.

6. Check if you missed weeding any piece, once you are done.

Applying Iron-On Vinyl

Before you decide to apply iron-on vinyl, you need to cut it first. Follow the steps below to cut your Cricut iron-on vinyl.

1. Log into your Design Space.

2.   Click on the Images tab on the left side of the panel and select an image from the huge library.

3.   After you have selected your image, they will appear in the canvas area.

4.   Click on the Edit Toolbar to resize appropriately to fit your project material.

5.   You can change the color of your image by clicking the ColorSync Panel in the upper layers panel on the left. Drag and drop the object into the layer of your desired color.

6.   Select Make It. A screen will pop up with a preview of your image.

7.   Since you are using iron-on vinyl, you must mirror it. When you click Mirror in the sidebar, your image will flip backwards on the mat.

8.   Click Continue and proceed to connect your computer to your Cricut Maker machine.

9.   Select your iron-on material from the list of materials.

10.   Flip your iron-on vinyl material back on your mat. Insert the mat into the Cricut machine and press the arrow button on it to hold your mat.

11.   Press the Go button and your Cricut maker will cut out your project.

12.   Press the arrow button again to release your mat.

After you are done cutting, the next thing is to weed it. We have shown you the tutorial on how to weed your iron-on vinyl.

Once you are done weeding, applying the vinyl on your material is next. Remember, you can use the Cricut EasyPress, normal iron, and a heat press to apply the iron-on vinyl on your material. We shall teach you how to use the whole three methods to adhere to your iron-on vinyl on your material.

Cricut EasyPress

Any size of EasyPress could be used to apply an iron-on vinyl on your material. Just make sure that you are using the one you are most comfortable with.

Before you transfer your design image to your material, you have to do a pre-press with your EasyPress for about 5 seconds. The aim is to flatten the material so that it can be ready for the design to be added.

You can decide to iron with your EasyPress directly on a plastic or anywhere that seems more convenient. Follow the process below.

1.   Press down with your EasyPress on the design image with steady pressure. Don't forget to put a plastic carrier sheet between your EasyPress and your vinyl.

2.   Press for some seconds and return to base to cool a bit.

3. Peel the back of the plastic carrier sheet if the vinyl sticks. If it doesn't, put the plastic back and press for some seconds again.

4. Remember to press the design image on your material front and back, with 10 – 15 seconds interval.

5. You have successfully used the EasyPress to apply your design image to your material.

Chapter 6 Cricut Software

Design Space

D esign Space is for any Explore machine with a high-speed, broadband Internet connection that is connected to a computer or an iOS device. This more advanced software allows full creative control for users with Cricut machines.

Craft Room

Some machines, such as the Explore and Explore Air, cannot use Craft Room, but many other models can. Craft Room users also have access to a free digital cartridge, which offers images that all Cricut machines can cut.

Moving on to Creating Your Project Template

On the home page, select "New Project", which will be followed by a page with a blank canvas that looks like the grid on your Cricut mats. To any artist, the words "empty canvas" is a nightmare in itself so please just bear with me since we will fill that bad boy up in a second. But first, let's go through the menu options.

New, Templates, Projects, Images, Text, Shapes, and Upload. These are the things that you will see on your left-hand side when you have the canvas open on the screen.

New

New means that you will start a new project and clicking the tab will redirect you to a blank canvas. Be sure to save all changes on your current project before you go to the new canvas. Otherwise, you will lose all of the progress you have already made on that design.

Templates

Clicking on Templates will allow you to set a template to help you visualize and work with sizing. It is very handy for someone who is not familiar with Cricut Design Space and doesn't know what sizes to set. If you are cutting out wearable items on fabric, you can change the size of the template to fit whoever will be wearing it. I'm sure you can agree that this feature is especially beneficial for the seamstresses out there.

Projects

Projects, meanwhile, will lead you to the ready-to-make projects so that you can start cutting right away. Some of the projects are not customizable, but others are when you open the template, which is pretty cool. Many of these are not free either, which irks me to a new extent. You can choose the "Free for Cricut (whatever machine you have)", and the projects that will turn up won't have to be paid for.

Images

Images are where you can search for thousands of photos to use for the craft. Those images with the green flag with the "A" on them are the ones that come only with Cricut Access so be aware if you do not have it. It is sort of like a Pinterest image search engine with a lot of pictures in its database.

Text

The Text basically goes without saying. When you select this option, you can type whatever you want and scale it onto your canvas. You may select any font saved in your computer too; that's why collecting those has never been more useful! There is also an option called "multi-layered font", which gives your text a shadow layer. If you are cutting out the letters and shadow layers, the Cricut will do them separately and combine the two later if you wish to. It can create very cool effects so make sure you try that option out. Furthermore, remember that when you are being paid to do a job, the font you are using might require a license to use.

Shapes

Shapes lets you add basic forms to your canvas, which you can tweak to fit your own needs. The shapes include circle, square, rectangle, triangle, et cetera.

Upload

When you click the Upload tab, you can upload your own images and transform them into cuttable pieces. This, along with the text, is the only reason why I still use Design Space. It is really awesome to be able to use this feature.

Cricut Basic

This is a program or software designed to help the new user get an easy start on designing new crafts and DIY projects. This system will help you with image selection to cutting with the least amount of time spent in the design stages. You can locate your image, pre-set projector font, and immediately print, cut, score, and align with tools that are found within the program. You can use this program on the iOS 7.1.2 or later systems as well as iPad and several of the iPhones from the Mini to the 5th generation iPod touch. Since it is also a cloud- based service, you are able to start in one device and finish from another.

Sure Cuts a Lot

This is another third-party software that has a funny name which gives you the ability to take control of your designs without some of the limitations that can happen when using cartridges used within the Cricut DesignStudio. You will need to install an update to your software to use this program; you can download it for free. It allows for the use of TrueType and OpenType font formats as well as simple drawing and editing tools. You can import any file format and then convert to the one that you need. There is an option for blackout and shadow.

Cricut DesignStudio

This program allows you to connect with your software and provides you with much more functionality as far as shapes and fonts are concerned. There are various options for tools that provide you resources for designing more creative images. You will be able to flip, rotate, weld, or slant the images and fonts. However, you will still be limited in the amounts or types of fonts that you can use based on the ones on the cartridges. There is a higher level of software features that allow for customization.

Cricut Sync

This is a program designed for updating the Cricut Expression 2 as well as the Imagine machine and the Gypsy device. You just connect your system to the computer and run the synced program for an installation of updates on the features that come with your machine. This is also used to troubleshoot many issues that could arise from the hardware.

Play Around and Practice

You can combine your shapes and images, add some text, and create patterns. The possibilities are endless. The best thing to do is familiarize yourself with the software before you attempt on cutting expensive materials. Start small and cheap - printer paper will be an ideal choice - and cut away. See what works well for you and stick with it. There are many options concerning the Cricut Design Space, and the only way to learn all of this is to experiment and click on every tab you see and try different combinations of options when playing around on the software.

Make the Cut

This is a third-party program that works with the Cricut design software. It offers a straightforward look at the design features that Cricut has. This system can convert a raster image into a vector so that you can cut it. There is also a great way to do lattice tools. It uses many file formats and TrueType fonts. There are advanced tools for editing and an interface that is easy to learn and use. This system works with Craft ROBO, Gazelle, Silhouette, Wishblade, and others. It allows you to import any file from a TTF, OTF, PDF, GSD, and so on and convert them to JPG, SVG, PDF, and so on. It is flexible and user-friendly.

Chapter 7 How to Earn Money With A Cricut Machine?

Just as a million Cricut machines can be used, you can make money from it.

Here are some ways to make money with a Cricut machine:

Create and sell leather bracelets

Bracelets are fashionable items, especially leather. The Cricut machine can easily cut real or artificial leather, which means less work. He decides to cut, make and sell leather bracelets because only the brooches, his Cricut machine, leather, and probably cardboard are the necessary materials.

If you are interested in selling this trade, you can also create a pre-release area where the buyer can hire the designer to create a specific project.

Sell Iron-On Wine and him

Another way to make money is with the Cricut machine. You create an iron vinyl design.

And sell to people. Iron vinyl can take the form of text or a pattern. You can also do it for any season or celebration, be it Valentine's Day, Halloween, Christmas, or Easter. Buyers can also order what they want.

Selling stickers

This idea is for children. You can make money by designing educational and entertainment stickers for toddlers and other ages. You can create alphabetical stickers or city maps. Stickers are also used to decorate places like a wardrobe or cupboard.

Create and sell parts and ornaments and banners

There is always a festival of people in our daily life. It can be a historic vacation or just a fun getaway. On this occasion, you can sell party decorations made with a Cricut machine.

Window stickers

They all have a strange image, an object that practically obsesses us. A sticker on a vinyl window of your favorite photo contributes significantly to your decor. Making and selling window stickers is fairly simple and inexpensive.

Create and sell wall screens

Personalized wall art would make money quickly and easily. Get inspirational quotes or designs and turn them into wall art for sale.

Design and sell the body

Bodies or combinations are usually charming fabrics that can be enhanced with amazing works of art. Baby combinations can be made with many other texts in addition to "Papa time" or " Mom baby ". Other sweet words can be used to design a children's costume.

Become a Cricut partner

That means paying for video tutorials for Cricut. These videos are sent to the Internet, which the Internet user can use. You need a strong Internet presence to become a Cricut partner. You must also have a visible number of subscribers in your social media accounts.

Post educational videos your vlog

It has nothing to do with being a partner. Instead, create a video blog, download video tutorials, and earn for the traffic you generate.

Use social media

You can do whatever crafts you find and post your photos online by indicating on the list that they are for sale. It works best because anyone shopping can see a picture of what they are getting before ordering. Non-standard handicrafts must also be included in the commercial order.

Design and sell t-shirts

Shirt is always fashionable clothes. A designed shirt would be a great fashion product, especially for students. I am making a shirt would generate income.

Design and sell sweatshirts

The sweatshirts are perfect for the cold season. Designed would be better in his youth. The project can also be ordered in advance.

Design and sell a piece of leather necklace

The leather pendant can be designed for a necklace and sold to interested buyers. You can also make and sell a piece of leather necklace.

Design and banners

Banners can be made for celebrations, holidays, camps, parties, religious events, or sports activities. All of this can be done and sold.

Design window attachment and sale

Seasonal window hangers can be made and sold. Other designs or images can also be used to create window stickers.

Design models and sales

Models can be created and sold for those who want to hand paint a message or brand. It would also bring a lot of money.

Design and sell stickers for safari animals

Safari animal stickers are attractive items. They can be sold and sold to animal lovers. The label is easy to make and will also be a source of income.

Design and sell stickers

You can create labels to mark things at home. Things in the kitchen, pantry, playroom, classroom and more

Places can be marked with stickers.

Design and sell Christmas decorations

Christmas is a time when people celebrate and decorate their work, their home, and their religion, among others.

Design and sell wipers

With the help of the machine, you can make a beautiful doormat and sell it to customers. It can be designed with text or images. Custom wipers may also be sold.

Design and sell rags

Towels used in the kitchen can be designed and sold at affordable prices. Towels can be designed with text or photos of delights.

Cricut offers countless options. Likewise, there are many things you can do that are negotiable. Independent entrepreneurship is easier than ever, thanks to the Internet and online platforms that facilitate the sale of your products.

You've probably heard of some platforms that make it easy to create your own store. Etsy is probably the most famous of these platforms and is setting up a store.

It's so simple that you can hardly be interested in starting your own!

Cricut, which creates countless objects of all kinds and themes for all occasions, is the name of the game. Creating these projects can be a great pleasure for an enthusiastic craftsman. However, when you spend money on materials for your projects, it pays to get a return depending on how much you earn and spend.

What are the best platforms to sell my Crafts?

This question is a bit stuffy and depends on the most convenient, convenient, and reliable platform for you. The business you want to start requires a lot of time and attention. Therefore, you should use a platform that meets all of your needs, meets all of your expectations, and solves more problems than it causes.

We can learn to forgive the quirks in the new systems if we learn them. Take a little more time to learn more about the experiences and opinions of people who have been using this platform for a long time. This gives you an idea of what your future might look like with this platform, and it is the only indicator to take into account to know-how

This platform will serve you.

You need to spend a little more time studying the platforms available, what the costs are (if any), how they treat their sellers, what percentage of their sales are made, and what the sellers think of those platforms.

Here are some of the best platforms you want to sign up for!

Etsy

Handmade amazon

Facebook market

Popular

Art fire

Arts and crafts

eBay

Craigslist

Chapter 8 Duel Cricut Tool Carriage

S o Which is the Best Cricut to Buy for Beginners?

Cricut producer stanzas cricut investigate for apprentices

So as should be obvious the entirety of the Cricut Machines utilize a similar plan programming. The entirety of the Cricuts additionally utilize a similar cut mats and similar controls. A similar fundamental strategy is utilized for cutting plans with each Cricut Machine.

It isn't so much that one Cricut machine is best for learners over another, it comes down to what you need your Cricut to do.

That said if you have the spending limit for it, the Cricut Maker can cut more materials. If you sew a ton it might simply be justified, despite all the trouble to have that rotating shaper. What's more, how cool is it to have wood patterns? Words cut in wood are excessively in vogue at this moment. Furthermore, who realizes what number of more instruments Cricut will turn out with that will just work in the Maker.

The advantage of purchasing a pack is you'll get all that you'll need or need to begin in one box. If you purchase a Cricut without anyone else you'll despite everything need to buy the apparatuses and supplies like vinyl before you can make anything.

A group will give you an examining of the different materials so you can begin creating immediately.

I'm certain you realize the art stores make them stun coupons. Be that as it may, don't get excessively energized, they all bar Cricut items, so you won't get any extra value reserve funds by heading off to the store.

This is an arrangement of inquiries I had when I purchased my Cricut. I genuinely wish I approached this kind of substance you are going to peruse. It would've made my life so a lot simpler!

These inquiries go from easy to progressively difficult. Hence you will become familiar with about this machine as you go!

few inquiries are much increasingly broad and they really require an additional post for it. So if there's a connect to one specific inquiry and you need to get familiar with that theme, simply snap to find out additional.

Cricut Maker Ready to Cut

A Cricut is a cutting machine and is a fantasy worked out as expected for some, crafters out there. You can utilize it for various different things like card making, home stylistic theme, and so forth.

Do you art or end up in a position where you have to cut a great deal? If the response to that is yes. Then you will absolutely profit by having a Cricut. Be that as it may, if you are not into sly things. Let's be honest! a Cricut can't you will truly profit by.

Are there different machines that can do something very similar?

Indeed! There are numerous different alternatives you can discover there that can do what the Cricut does somewhat.

In the market, there are two other significant brands that additionally cut an extraordinary assortment of materials and that likewise has incredible audits.

Is the Cricut better than different machines out there?

I accept each kick the bucket cutting machine is stunning.

That says that regardless of what machine you pick you will completely adore it

Here's the other thing. Because I happen to have a Cricut and I love it, I won't diss on different brands or machines.

Cricut happens to be the pass on slicing machine brand I chose to go to with. So essentially all you see here will be towards this specific brand.

For what reason Should I pick Cricut over different brands?

Because it's the one you need.

A few people will say they abhor it, others will say they love it. Be that as it may, by the day's end, the cash is leaving your pocket. So you ought to pick what you are increasingly alright with.

I for one imagine that Provo Craft and Novelty – the organization that made this astounding instrument – is a flawless organization and you can see and feel the nature of their items. You realize that all that they make is made with adoration.

One of different things I have preferred about this machine, and that I really discovered after I got it is that the Cricut is in excess of a shaper!

There's the Cricut Community. You can get huge amounts of thoughts and free instructional exercises on the web. We creatives love sharing tips and deceives on the most proficient method to exploit this excessively cool device.

For what reason did I get a Cricut?

Not excessively this inquiry matters to you. In any case, this is the principle reason I got one, and you may feel enlivened by it!

I recall a discussion with my relative where I was asking her what should I blog about. She realizes I make and structure beautiful things for practically any event.

Subsequent to giving me huge amounts of thoughts; She prescribed me to find out about the Cricut!

What are the accessible Cricut Machines out there?

I am going to separate this for you without any problem! At this moment you there are 3 different models of Cricut Machines accessible:

• Cricut Explore Mint and Cricut Maker Rose

• Cricut Explore Left – Cricut Maker Right

Cricut Explore Family: These are the most well-known machines with initially three decisions to look over. These three machines can cut similar materials, however every one of them has different highlights.

Cricut Explore One and Explore Air: Were the main forms of the Explore Air 2. The first had just one apparatus holder and the subsequent one had two instrument holders and Bluetooth association. Note: You can get them utilized, Cricut never again sells them on its site.

Cricut Explore Air 2: Has similar capacities, that the investigate air (cuts, draws, scores, print then cut) however it's multiple times quicker.

Cricut Maker: This machine is more impressive than the Explore Air 2 as it permits you to cut with 10X the quality. With the Maker, you can cut, score, deboss, and that's only the tip of the iceberg!

Cricut Joy: it's the most up to date machine Cricut discharged. It's tenny little and it can cut, draw a wide assortment of materials. the Cricut Joy can cut and draw vinyl and iron-on without a tangle!

Cricut Joy machine with pen introduced.

Cricut Joy

There were different machines accessible also (counting the Cricut Cuddlebug).

You may have the option to buy them on amazon or utilized. Notwithstanding, they are not good with Cricut Design Space and the product they utilized before – Cricut Craft Room – has been closed down totally.

Is the Cricut excessively costly?

Directly off bat let me disclose to you that YES a Cricut machine can be very costly.

Notwithstanding, notice I state that it very well may be. This is because if you take a gander at a portion of the primary machines you can see that there are great arrangements and you can begin when you need.

The most economical machine is the Cricut Cuttlebug – A modest yet beyond words machine – and the Most costly alternative is for their most recent discharge, The Cricut Maker.

Is the Cricut justified, despite all the trouble?

This is so factor and it needs to do about your side interests, needs and furthermore your spending limit.

If you create once per year, listen to me you DON'T require a Cricut. Notwithstanding, if making and making stuff is your jam then a Cricut merits each penny.

Is having a Cricut going to profit you and make your life sufficiently simple to spare time – time is cash – and simply make your life increasingly charming?

If your answer is YES: Then GO pull the trigger.

I am not the sort of individual that purchases everything. Be that as it may, here and there when I weight the upsides and downsides. I simply let it all out.

What is the best Cricut I can get?

The best Cricut you can get, pass on it's the Cricut Maker.

It's their most up to date discharge and they are thinking of numerous apparatuses that will make cutting and creating very simple and way progressively pleasant. As it were, the Cricut Maker is a definitive Crafter's fantasy.

What is the best Cricut for me?

The best Cricut you can get is the one that meets these 3 things:

• The one you can manage.

• The one you can slice the materials you need to cut.

• The one that will leave you with save cash to purchase materials (often disregarded).

Above all else, I was unable to bear the cost of the creator. Second of all – as of now in life – I am just keen on cutting paper, vinyl and some texture to a great extent. Also, to wrap things up, what is the purpose of having an increasingly costly machine if you don't have the cash to purchase additional materials to work with?

Notwithstanding, if you haven't purchased a machine and you truly need to cut wood and texture I believe is smarter to do the speculation now, and afterward get additional instruments and materials as you go.

Update: Eventually I got the Cricut Maker too because I needed to show all of you the potential outcomes with the two machines.

Would it be a good idea for me to redesign my Cricut?

If you as of now have a Cricut machine let me reveal to you something – You ROCK!

Is it true that you are thinking about overhauling? I feel you.

After I purchased my Explore Air 2 I felt insufficient, all the instructional exercises are currently for the Maker, and that I should simply update.

Do you overhaul your telephone, vehicle, and other electronic gadgets consistently? I sure don't. So – except if I am given one – until I abuse each and every chance and I am prepared to learn different methods. I won't overhaul my machine.

Shouldn't something be said about you?

Would you like to overhaul because you need the most current form? Or on the other hand, would you like to update because you really exceeded your present machine?

If you said yes to the second and have the spending limit for it! Welcome to the Cricut Maker family! I am in no uncertainty that you will see this machine as an extraordinary fit for you

Cricut has things on Sale practically constantly.

You can discover great ones during the special seasons and on unique events. A few retailers additionally run incredible limits. Indeed, I see huge amounts of them on Facebook.

Where would i be able to locate the best deals and arrangements for the Cricut?

If I were going to buy a Cricut right now I would do it from their Official Website. They simply have incredible limits accessible constantly.

Here you can discover extraordinary arrangements on groups, machines, and materials.

What materials would i be able to cut with the Cricut?

There are hundreds – actually – of materials you can cut with these stunning machine these are some of them:

• Plan Paper

• A wide range of cardstock

• Metallic Paper

• Vinyl (Iron on, sparkle, lasting, removable)

• Texture and materials

• Artificial Leather

- Creased Paper

- Meager Woods (Cricut Maker as it were)

- Sticker Paper

- Material Paper

Chapter 9 Cricut Machine Maintenance & Troubleshooting

Blade Life

A blade can last between 500 and 1500 single cuts before it requires replacement. The life expectancy for a cutting blade mostly relies on the settings you use and the materials you cut. This is why you need to monitor the quality of your cuts, and when the quality decreases, that's when you will need to replace your cutting blade. In order to have the best possible results, make sure you only use Cricut Replacement Cutting Blades, available on the Cricut Shop, but also at other retailers.

Replacing the Cutting Blade

This is a process that you will definitely come across, especially if you are using the Cricut Machine on a frequent basis. Never replace the blade when the Cricut Machine is still on, in fact, you need to unplug it before replacing the cutting blade. After the machine is unplugged, you will need to take out the cutting blade assembly. Then, you will need to find the blade in the assembly and push it in, in order for the blade to emerge from the cutting blade assembly. Next, you will need to gently pull out the blade from the magnet that is holding it in place.

When you need to install a new blade, you will need to let go of the blade release and insert with caution the shaft of the blade in the hole at the bottom of the cutting blade assembly. Then, you will notice how the blade gets "sucked" inside the shaft and installed properly. Place back the cutting blade assembly into the Cricut Machine following the reversed procedure of removing the cutting blade assembly. Please be aware that the cutting blades are very sharp and should only be handled with extra care. Also, they can be considered choking hazards, so you need to keep them away from children.

Replacing the Cutting Mat

Nothing lasts forever and the Cricut Cutting Mat doesn't make any exception from this rule. It takes between 25 and 40 full cuts for a Cutting Mat to get damaged and at that point, it should be replaced. The life expectancy of this spare part depends a lot on the materials you cut and the settings you use. When the paper is no longer sticking to the Cutting Mat, it has to be replaced. It's always better to replace the mat with genuine Cricut Mats, and it's perfect if you can purchase the Cricut Self Healing Mat. Always remember to rotate the mats to prolong the overall life of each mat.

Cleaning and Greasing Your Cricut Machine

Every product can show signs of usage, and a Cricut Machine may collect some paper particles and dust, or you can even see grease from the machine building up in the carriage track. Luckily for you, cleaning up this machine is quite easy, but you need to consider the following tips first:

- Make sure you unplug the power from the machine first before cleaning it

- You can use a glass cleaner sprayed on a soft cloth to clean the machine

- If you notice static electricity build up leading to the accumulation of paper particles and dust, all you have to do is to wipe it off with a clean soft cloth

- If you see grease building up on the bar across which the carriage travels, gently remove it using a soft cloth, tissue, or cotton swab

Machine Dial Not Working

If you ever come across issues with dialing on your Cricut Machine, you can just follow the troubleshooting steps below

When Explore Smart Set Dial won't turn:

- In this case, you will need to look for your proof of purchase (any receipt or invoice your might have regarding the purchase of this product) and prepare a short video of the issue

- You will need to Contact Member Care, using one of the options for assistance

- Unfortunately, there is no way to troubleshoot this issue

- When the material is not changing in Design Space:

- Check the connection of the USB cable on both your Cricut machine and your computer.

- Unplug the Cricut machine from the computer and then power it off. Next step, reboot or restart your computer. When the computer is back on, turn on the Cricut machine and reconnect it to the computer, then try to see if it's cutting again. If it still doesn't work, make sure you try the following step.

- Consider reconnecting your Cricut machine through a different USB port on your computer. If it still doesn't help, move on to the next step.

- Check if the issue happens with a different Internet browser. If the issue is happening regardless of the browser you are using, please consider the next step.

- Try to see if a different USB cable works (if you have a standard printer you can try it with that cable and vice versa), just to see if the Cricut machine can cut with a different cable. If your machine is in warranty and you don't have another cable, you might want to consider contacting Member Care.

- Check for any possible updates (make sure the Firmware is updated) on your Cricut Machine.

- If there are no available updates, please get in touch withMember Care for further assistance.

Machine Tearing or Dragging Materials

There might be situations when the machine has some malfunctions and it tears through the material. However, all these variables can be fixed using some basic troubleshooting steps. Therefore, if your Cricut machine is dragging or tearing through the material, make sure you check the following:

1. Check if you selected the right material setting in Design Space, or make sure that Smart Set Dial is on the right setting:

    a. if you are making a Custom setting, you can make sure that you select the right material from the drop-down menu

2. Check the intricacy and size of the image. When you are cutting an image that is small or very intricate, try cutting it larger or simpler.

    a. If cutting a simple image fixes the issue, you can try cutting the more complicated one by using the Custom setting for Cardstock - Intricate Cuts.

    b. If you are using Cricut Maker or Cricut Explore Air 2 in Fast Mode, make sure you disable the Fast Mode and reattempt the cut again.

3. Take off the blade housing from the machine, then the blade and make sure there isn't any debris on the blade or inside the housing.

4. Decrease pressure settings for that specific material type in the Manage Custom Materials window by increments of 2-4. You can access the Manage Custom Materials screen from the account menu, or by going to the Edit Custom Materials option from the upper right corner of the Mat Preview screen (just after clicking on Change Material).

5. It may have to be done 2-3 times in order to change the cut result.

6. Try to cut a different material (I would suggest copy paper) using the right setting for that material. Try to see if the problem is only with the material that you are trying to cut, or the issue persists with other materials as well.

7. Consider using a new mat and blade. In this case, both of them can cause cut issues.

8. If you followed all the steps above, but the issues still persist, I encourage you to get in touch with Member Care for further assistance.

Machine Not Cutting Through Material

One of the most common issues of any Cricut machine is when it simply doesn't cut through the material, or it's just scoring the material, even though it normally should be cut without issues if it has the right settings applied. In this case, you only need to follow the troubleshooting steps below:

1. Check if the material setting you chose in Design Space or on Smart Set Dial matches the material on your machine mat. If you are using Cricut Explore models, you can go ahead with the Custom option, and then select the right material from the Custom Materials list.

2. Go to the account menu and open the Manage Custom Materials page, and from this option, raise the pressure for your material setting by 2-4 increments. After this, try a test cut. You may have to increase the pressure settings by 2-4 increments 2-3 times, to check if there are any changes in the cut result.

3. Try cutting a different material (the best choice would be printer paper), but using the right setting for the material. Do you still have the same issue? If not, then perhaps the issue lies within the original material you are trying to cut.

4. On your browser, you can also clear the cache and cookies, and then try another test cut, and if the issue persists, may I

suggest trying a different browser (I normally recommend Google Chrome or Mozilla Firefox).

5. If you have attempted all of the steps above, and you still have issues, please get in touch with Member Care for further assistance.

Chapter 10 Definitions Associated with the Cricut Maker

There are several words that are uniquely associated with the Cricut Maker and then there are some words that mean something completely different than the usual meaning when used in conjunction with your Cricut Maker. For example, the word "attach" is a tool in our definitions, but Webster defines this different. The word makes sense as you do use the attach tool to keep things in place, but the definition is not what you would expect "attach" to be. This is why we created the definitions section:

Attach – The attach tool is located in Design Space. If you decide to purchase Design Space, you will use the attach tool. This is the tool that helps to hold your cuts in place on your cutting mat in the design screen. It also helps to fasten a score layer to cut a layer after you score it.

Contour – The contour tool is also a feature you can use in Design Space. As this guide has demonstrated, Design Space is used often. Contour removes unwanted cut lines and is therefore very useful for beginners, especially.

Compound Path – This is a term used to define when all the cut lines are grouped together. You can also edit the compound lines by grouping the compound paths together and the right-click to release the compound path.

Cut Lines – This is the same term that is used with a basic sewing pattern and the symbol scissors is marked on the pattern. The cut lines are where the shape is supposed to be cut. These lines are either red or gray and this is where your Cricut Make will cut whatever it is you are cutting. These lines are also where your pens will draw if you are drawing or writing.

Decal - A decal is the product you have after you finish cutting shapes from vinyl.

Design Space – This is the program your guide has been talking so much about. There are many projects and fonts you can access in Design Space. Design Space is pretty necessary for the Cricut Maker to do everything it needs to do.

Firmware – Firmware is a program that is already on your Cricut Maker. Updates will occur when you plug your Cricut Maker into your laptop.

Floating Panels – These panels are used so you can work in different areas at the same time. You can cut in one area while designing in another.

Force – Force is the amount of pressure you apply with the blade to the thickness of the material you are using. This ensures a complete and sharp cut regardless of how thick the material might be.

Group/Ungroup – To group or Ungroup is a command that helps you to do just what this action says it does. You are able to combine several layers or images together. This even allows you to combine multiple layers of text together. In reverse action, this command allows you to ungroup a set of layers or images. They will then be able to move independently of each other.

Heat Transfer Vinyl – Remember when you had to have numbers or letters put on the back of shirts by an outside company? With a Cricut Maker, you are able to use a specialty vinyl that can be used on fabrics to create those designs. This vinyl comes with an adhesive backing and a sheet so it can be cut just right to fit on the fabric.

Kiss cut – Kiss cut is a very precise cut made that only cuts through one layer. It is a thin top layer usually cut when making a decal.

Mirrored Image – A mirrored image is the reverse of any image. Most of the iron-on materials have to be mirrored. The software will tell you when to turn on the mirror image tool. This is used in Design Space and is something you use before doing your cuts.

Offset – Often when people think of offset, they think of an offset press as in printing. This is much like a printing press function. You choose the distance you want around the border of any design. It can be a predesign or a design of your own. The offset function is used often in sign making.

Print then Cut – The print then cut feature is what allows you to print from your computer to your home printer. Then the Cricut can die cut the design.

Printable Vinyl – Printable vinyl is vinyl that can be sent through the home printer and then the Cricut is able to die cut it. It is also called a print and cut function.

Reverse Weeding – Reverse weeding is when you remove vinyl that is left behind after you make stencils or other cuts.

Scraper – The scraper is sometimes called a squeegee. This is a flat tool that is used to smoothen out transfer tape and other thin material like decals.

Sketching – Sketching is the same thing as drawing, only this action is done by your machine with any of the pens. You can use the pen included with the machine or buy extra pens from Cricut or use pens from any pen section. Some will work better than others. Just experiment with this fun activity.

Slice – The slice action and tool create a new path from two images. This will result in completely new images or shapes. They should show up in the layers panel as individual layers.

Spatula – You will use a spatula often once you are more familiar with the Cricut Maker. This is a tool used to remove smaller pieces of vinyl or paper from mats after you have made cuts

SVG – SVG files are files that are used in the Cricut Maker. These are traced images that can be made larger or smaller and they do not lose resolution.

Teflon – Teflon is a thin waxy sheet that is used when ironing. This Teflon is used to protect your iron or your heat press. Just like the Teflon on a pan, this sturdy, but thin material stands up to heat and makes it possible for you do use heat for your projects.

Text to Path – When you do text to path, this is an action of moving the text to curve it around a pattern or a shape like a square or a circle.

Transfer Tape – Transfer tape is a special tape that is used to move adhesive vinyl from the carrier sheet to the surface of whatever kind of project you are working on.

Weeding – When you are weeding, think of the process you used in your garden, only transfer that to removing unwanted vinyl from a decal.

Weeding lines – Weeding lines are the cut lines that make it easier to cut out a project, aka, weeding.

Weld – The weld tool allows you to join shapes to create a single object.

ZIP File – A ZIP file is a compressed or smaller-sized file containing one or more files. You will need to unzip the file to get access to the contents by right-clicking the ZIP and clicking "Extract all...". macOS users can unzip a zip file by double-clicking the file or moving it to the desktop and then double-clicking the file.

Chapter 11 Projects and Ideas with Paper

C ricut projects. It's definitely the cheapest and easiest to find among all the materials. Cardstock is usually the first choice, as it's sturdy and can handle a lot of folding, cutting, and art supplies. There are hundreds of thousands of varieties of paper, though, and you can experiment to see what you like best. The types of paper listed for each project is merely a suggestion. Paper also has the advantage of working well in every Cricut machine.

With paper, in particular, you'll want to make sure your blade is sharp and clean. Anything out of the ordinary will tear the paper. Dull blades are the biggest culprit when you find tears in your paper. Make sure you're using the appropriate blade for the weight of the paper as well. Some thicker papers might just need a second pass rather than a sharper blade. It's good to have some spare paper that you can do test runs with.

If you're using a new cutting mat, you'll need to condition it before you put your paper on it. New mats are very sticky, and you won't be able to get the paper off again without tearing it. Conditioning is quick and easy, though. Simply touch the mat with your hands. The oils on your skin will decrease the stickiness without damaging your mat. Touch repeatedly until mat feels less sticky, and make sure to get all of the edges and corners. Test the mat with some scrap paper before using it for your project.

Paper can be found at just about any store. However, some specialty stores and websites will actually give you a cheat sheet on how to cut their different papers with different cutting machines. You might find a list of all of their papers and which blades and settings to use for them. Some will even offer instructions for creating a custom material for specific papers. Check out the help section of specialty paper websites to see if they have this.

The Cricut machines don't just cut paper; they can also write and draw. Cricut offers a wide selection of different pens, and there are other brands that will fit in the machine as well. A couple of the following projects take advantage of this feature, but you can incorporate it into the others as well. You can draw or write anything on any of your patterns. With the Cricut Explore One and Cricut Explore Air 2, you'll need to swap out pens if you want to change colors. The Cricut Maker has two tool carriages, so you can do at least two colors at once without swapping.

Paper Bouquet

Flowers are nice, but it doesn't take long for them to wilt. How about some paper ones instead? They'll last you forever! Use this bouquet as décor in your home or for an event. Budget-conscious brides can even carry this down the aisle instead of an expensive floral arrangement! You will find plenty of templates in the Cricut Design Space for different flowers. You can also search online for more, or you can try your hand at making your own. A bouquet can be made up of one type of flower, the same flower in different colors, a variety of flowers, or a variety of flowers, all in the same color. It depends on the look and feel that you are going for, so use whatever method sounds best to you. You can use plain cardstock, patterned cardstock, or use watercolor to create a color gradient you love. For the stems, pipe cleaners are easier to work with and can be covered with tissue paper or something similar. Or, it can be left visible for a crafty look. The floral wire will give a more realistic look, but it's thinner and takes some work. You can use the Cricut Explore One, Cricut Explore Air 2, or Cricut Maker for this project.

Supplies Needed

- Cardstock

- Glue gun

- Lightstick cutting mat

- Weeding tool or pick

- Green pipe cleaners or floral wire

1. **Directions:**

2. Open Cricut Design Space and create a new project.

3. Select the "Image" button in the lower left-hand corner and search for "paper flowers."

4. Select the image with several flower pieces and click "Insert."

5. Copy the flowers and resize for variety in your bouquet.

6. Place your cardstock on the cutting mat.

7. Send the design to your Cricut.

8. Remove the outer edge of the paper, leaving the flowers on the mat.

9. Use your weeding tool or carefully pick to remove the flowers from the mat.

10. Glue the flower pieces together in the centers, with the largest petals at the bottom.

   a. Bend or curl petals as desired to create multiple looks.

   b. Glue the flowers to the ends of the pipe cleaners or sections of floral wire.

   c. Gather your flowers together in a vase or wrap them with tissue paper.

   d. Enjoy your beautiful bouquet!

Leafy Garland

Garlands are an easy way to spruce up any space, and there is an infinite variety of them. Create a unique leafy one to give your home a more naturalistic feel! Feel free to change the colors of the leaves to suit you, whether you stick with green or go a little more unnatural. Tweaking the size of the bundles you make and how close you put them together will change the look of the garland. You can use different types of leaves as well. Experiment a little bit to see what you like best. Bending the leaves down the center and curling the edges a little will give you a more realistic look, or you can leave them flat for a handmade look. You can use the Cricut Explore One, Cricut Explore Air 2, or Cricut Maker for this project.

Supplies Needed

- Cardstock – 2 or more colors of green, or white to paint yourself

- Glue gun

- Lightstick cutting mat

- Weeding tool or pick

- Floral wire

- Floral tape

Directions:

1. Open Cricut Design Space and create a new project.

2. Select the "Image" button in the lower left-hand corner and search for "leaf collage."

3. Select the image of leaves and click "Insert."

4. Place your cardstock on the cutting mat.

5. Send the design to your Cricut.

6. Remove the outer edge of the paper, leaving the leaves on the mat.

7. Use a pick or scoring tool to score down the center of each leaf lightly.

8. Use your weeding tool or carefully pick to remove the leaves from the mat.

9. Gently bend each leaf at the scoreline.

   a. Glue the leaves into bunches of two or three.

b. Cut a length of floral wire to your desired garland size, and wrap the ends with floral tape.

c. Attach the leaf bunches to the wire using the floral tape.

d. Continue attaching leaves until you have a garland of the size you want. Bundle lots of leaves for a really full look, or spread them out to be sparser.

e. Create hooks at the ends of the garland with floral wire.

f. Hang your beautiful leaf garland wherever you'd like!

Easy Envelope Addressing

Christmas cards are wonderful to send out, but they can take forever to address. Address labels just don't look as personal, though. Use the Cricut pen tool in your machine to "hand letter" your envelopes! You can use this for your batch of holiday cards or even for other cards or letters. This takes advantage of the writing function of your Cricut machine. For the most realistic written look, make sure you select a font in the writing style. It will still write other fonts, but it will only create an outline of them, which is a different look you could go for! Cricut offers a variety of Pen Tools, and there are some other pens that will fit as well. For addressing envelopes, stick to black or another color that is easy to read so that the mail makes it to its destination. You can use the Cricut Explore One, Cricut Explore Air 2, or Cricut Maker for this project.

Supplies Needed

- Envelopes to address

- Cricut Pen Tool

- Lightstick cutting mat

Directions:

1. Open Cricut Design Space and create a new project.

2. Create a box the appropriate size for your envelopes.

3. Select the "Text" button in the lower left-hand corner.

4. Choose one handwriting font for a uniform look or different fonts for each line to mix it up.

5. Type your return address in the upper left-hand corner of the design.

6. Type the "to" address in the center of the design.

7. Insert your Cricut pen into the auxiliary holder of your Cricut, making sure it is secure.

8. Place your cardstock on the cutting mat.

9. Send the design to your Cricut.

    a. Remove your envelope and repeat as needed.

    b. Send out your "hand-lettered" envelopes!

Conclusion

Cricut machines are awesome gadgets to own because they do not only boost creativity and productivity, they can also be used to create crafts for business. With Design Space, crafters can create almost anything, and even customize their products to bear their imprints.

All over the world, people use these machines to make gift items, t-shirts, interior décor, and many other crafts, to beautify their homes, share with friends and family during holidays, and even sell, etc.

There two types of Cricut machines; the Cricut Explore and the Cricut Maker. Both machines are highly efficient in their rights, and experts in the crafting world make use of them to create a plethora of items, either as a hobby or for business.

Both machines are similar in many ways i.e. the Cricut Maker and the Explore Air 2, but the Cricut Maker is somewhat of a more advanced machine because it comes with some advanced features, as compared to the Explore Air 2.

One distinct feature about the Maker that sets it apart from the Explore Air is the fact that it can cut thicker materials. With the Maker, the possibilities are limitless and crafters can embark on projects that were never possible with Cricut machines before the release of the Make.

Another feature that puts the Cricut Maker machine ahead of the Explore Air 2 is the 'Adaptive Tool System'. With this tool, the Cricut Maker has been empowered in such a way that it will remain relevant for many years to come because it will be compatible to new blades and other accessories that Cricut will release in the foreseeable future.

Although both machines have several dissimilarities, there are also areas where they completely inseparable. Take for example the designing of projects in Cricut Design Space.

Cricut Design Space is the software where all the magnificent designs are made before they are sent to be cut. It is one of the most important aspects in the creation of crafts in the Cricut set up. However, when it comes to Cricut Maker and the Explore Air 2, there is nothing to separate them in this regard, because both machines use the same software for project design.

As a crafter, without proper knowledge of Design Space, you're not only going to cut out poor products, you will also make little or no in-road in your quest to find success.

Understanding Design Space is important because it empowers crafters with enormous tools and materials to create generalized and custom products. It is an extremely powerful tool that just cannot be overlooked by anyone that intends to follow this path.

Thus, the understanding of Design Space is a MUST for people that intend to make a business out of Cricut machines or even utilize it as a hobby. With the software, crafters can create their designs from scratch or use already-made designs on the Cricut platform. Those that have an active subscription on Cricut Access, have access to thousands of images, projects, and fonts. They can cut out their products using these images or projects, and they can also edit them to suit their style and taste before cutting.

Cricut Design Space comes with some exciting tools and features that can make crafting easy and straightforward. These tools are not so hard to use, thus, in order to get conversant with them, you need to do some research and consistently apply the knowledge you gain from your research and reading. Expert crafters know all about the important tools in Cricut Design Space, as well as the role they play in the design of projects. Some of these tools include; the slice tool, weld tool, contour tool, attach tool and flatten tool, etc.

Cricut machines do not function separately -when you purchase them, they come with accessories and tools that are required for them to function. Minus the tools and accessories that come in the pack, there are also others can be purchased separately in order to boost the machine's functionality and output. Basic accessories and tools that are needed for crafters to use along with their machines for optimum functionality and ease of design and production.

In terms of the Cricut Design Space software and app, some tips and tricks aid the process of project design and production. The software is easy and straightforward to learn and design on, but like every other applications and software, it still has some related issues and problems.

When problems arise, solutions are naturally proffered, and in terms of Cricut Design Space, there are several ways to address app related issues to improve user experience and functionality.

The Design Space software is web based, thus, some laptop computers are perfectly suited for the purpose. These laptops are suitable for several reasons, including; speed, Space and design, etc. In summary, the best five are; Asus Vivobook F510UA, Dell Inspiron 15 5575, Lenovo Ideapad 330S, Asus Vivobook S410UN, and the Acer Aspire E 15.

Everything on earth needs maintenance, including Cricut machines. These machines are constantly cutting out materials of different textures, shapes, and quantity, etc. Thus, they need routine maintenance in order to boost their productivity levels and increase their life span.

The routine maintenance of these machines does not require a lot, and as a matter of fact, the hardware needs cleaning after cutting out materials. Thus, non-alcoholic baby wipes are highly recommended for cleaning material residue on the machines. The cutting mat is another item that needs maintenance from time to time because excessive usage without proper care reduces its stickiness.

In terms of projects, there are so many items that can be designed, and cut out from Cricut machines.

Also, these items can be sold in the crafts market for profit. Although some people use the machines for recreational purposes, there are even a higher number of people that use to for commercial purposes.

Commercial users of Cricut machines design and cut out items to sell for profit and the machines have proven to be a blast.

One of the reasons why people can sell items made from Cricut machine is because they have the option of creating custom and unique products that cannot be found anywhere else.

Cricut machines are awesome tools that should be on everybody's radar, especially people that love crafts.

CRICUT PROJECT IDEAS FOR BEGINNERS

The Best Project Ideas to Create Your Cricut Object and Spark Your Imagination with pictures and illustrations to guide you during the process

Emily Maker

Introduction

We should not forget that the cool thing about Cricut is that projects are endless. You might decide to have your own wall lettering, or you might choose to make a nursery at home, and you would need to make that distinct wall painting with several letters. Instead of you to spend several hours cutting with blades and carving with knives or any other cutting device, you just need a Cricut machine. You don't even need to hire a muralist for your hand painting because you can do that yourself. In fact, people like these are happy that you are not exposed to this knowledge so that they can make some cash from you. The die cut machine produces those precise cuts which children and other professional needs. There are several die-cut stickers you can get from this machine. This machine also allows you to render wedding favors and party favors easily by helping in the creating process of tags, bags, boxes, and several other party creations. These pieces can come in several forms like gift bags, banners, hats, etc. these and many more can fit the theme of any party because you are making them. As much as I would love to shy away from the scrapbook stuff I just can't. Now, just picture your daughter or your son getting married and you present him/her with a scrapbook having pictures from the very first day they stepped into this planet to where they are now. Gifts like this sound odd, but they are invaluable because you are not giving out a utensil or a tool you are giving out those memories. Scrapbooks carry out a lot of memories and those feelings you cannot give through your regular gifts.

We shouldn't forget that the Vinyl is another material which you need to make your work on the Cricut machine smooth. The Cricut machine can work on those beautiful materials which can be used to make decals, stencils, graphics, and those beautiful signs too. You can cut through the following vinyl materials; chalkboard vinyl, dry erase vinyl, holographic vinyl, stencil vinyl, printable vinyl, Matte Vinyl, Adhesive Vinyl, Printable Vinyl, and Glossy Vinyl also. Furthermore, you may have so much experience in the fabric and Textile world, and you want to infuse the Cricut machine. Some of the materials or fabrics that you can work with are; canvas, denim, cotton fabric, linen, leather, flannel, burlap, duck cloth, felt, metallic leather, polyester, printable fabrics, silk, wool felt and many more others. If you have not got your Iron on Vinyl. Which is meant to be the heat transfer vinyl. You make use of this vinyl to decorate a T-shirt, tote bags and other kind of fabric items that you can think of like; Printable Iron On, Glitter Iron on, Glossy Iron On, Flocked Iron on, Holographic sparkle iron on, Metallic Iron on, Neon Iron on, Foil Iron on, etc.

We should not narrow our minds to the materials mentioned above because there are several other materials which the Cricut can cut through or even work on some of them include; adhesive wood, cork board, Balsa Wood, craft foam, aluminum sheets, corrugated paper, Embossable foil, Foil Acetate, Paint Chips, Plastic Packaging, Metallic

Vellum, Printable Sticker Paper, Stencil material, Shrink Plastic, Wrapping Paper, Window Cling, Wood Veneer, Washi Tape, Birch Wood, Wrapping Paper, Wood Veneer, Plastic Packaging, Soda Can, Glitter Foam, Printable Magnet Sheets, etc. The Cricut maker can work on materials which are up to 2.4mm thick and other special materials and special fabrics like the; Jersey, Cashmere, Chiffon, Terry Cloth, Tweed, Velvet, Jute, Knits, Moleskin, Fleece, and several others.

This machine can be found anywhere and everywhere, so much paper artwork is done. What this suggests is that you can see these machines in schools, offices, craft shops, etc. you can make use of this Cricut machine for a school project, card stock projects as well as iron-on projects too. Making use of this machine to cut out window clings is not a bad idea at all. It is not limited to this because you also engage in projects that have to do with adhesive stencil and stencil vinyl also. You would remove the stencil vinyl after it is dried. This would leave a distinct imprint. You can also make use of this machine to create lovely fashion accessories like several pieces of jewelry. The Cricut machine allows you to make use of the faux leather for exceptional designs. Recall that we talked about school projects. Preschoolers and their instructors can benefit from this machine. Furthermore, you can print out photos or images from your computer while making use of this machine, especially from the printable magnets to those sticker papers, customized gifts, bags, etc.

Defining objects requires you to use other similar objects to drive home your point and to give the reader a clearer picture. The very available way we can describe a Cricut machine is to say that it is a machine that has so much resemblance with the printer, but it is used majorly for cutting designed pieces. That is a very simple and easy definition you don't need to bother yourself about that. Just picture a printer in your mind and think of a cutting device. Oh, no, you already have the Cricut machine with you, right? You would notice that it uses precise blades and several templates or rollers during cutting.

Against what people think. The machine isn't meant for scrapbook keepers or makers alone. I still don't know why this idea has become so much rooted in the minds of people that we've grown to allow this thought to dominate our reactions and attitude towards any new innovation.

The world has been transformed with that machine as its products have been able to add those special visual beauties to the simple paperwork that we know. The Cricut machine has several models and versions some of them include; Cricut Expression, Expression 2, Cricut Imagine, Cricut Gypsy, Cricut Cake Mini, Cricut Personal Cutter, Cricut Crafts Edition and Martha Stewart and the Cricut Explore air. The tool obviously fits into any type of craft you are working on. And there is also a die cut machine which gives you that extra-precise, sharp and smart cutting. The process of cutting materials by hand during crafts has been reduced drastically, thanks to this wonderful machine. More also, you can perform multiple projects all at the same time due to the effectiveness of this device. It contains several cartridges which are always available to help you explore different forms and shapes of several designs. More also that move from one project to another has been made possible with the use of this Cricut machine.

Any material can be shaped into that design you want it to be. Furthermore, you can also create patterns which are already pre-installed in the software that comes with it. The design software tool becomes very much available with pre-loaded designs for instant use. I am sure you must have been able to purchase this machine from your local craft store on the online store. You are aware that the price was based on the kind of model you are using and I am sure that you've been able to narrow down your needs for you to be able to get your machine because anything which makes your work easier and faster is a very important investment and the Cricut machine is definitely one. Due to the efficiency of this machine, we now have it in several places we never thought it would be in years. We have them in offices and specific workshops. If you think that the Cricut is a home-only tool, you are quite wrong. This time-saving device allows your work to be very professional, and the beautiful thing about it is that we have no limits to what it can do. I am sure that you're reading this to gain more ideas and you hastily want to jump into making things and doing some stuff. Yes, that is cool; however, we need to understand some basics else we would be making serious mistakes or the process would look very confusing.

The machine has lineages, and I am sure you are aware of that. It wasn't like this some years back but who really cares about the past more than the future. Remember we have the Cricut maker which is this cloud-based online software having this particular series and design which obviously cannot function alone because it has to be attached with the desktop or laptop computer having an available internet connection. But today, this Cricut maker has several offline features present in that design app which has so much compatibility with several devices like the iOS device and Windows also. What this suggests is that if you have this kind of machine you can work without the use of any internet connection, and you can also make use of an iPad/iPhone or Macbook. This general feature is also included in the Cricut Explore Air, but the difference is that you don't need a connection through a cable because you already have a Bluetooth connection in place.

Chapter 1 What is a Cricut Machine?

The cricut maker machine is an electronic die-cutter for different materials including papers, vinyl and fabrics into desired shapes and patterns. This machine is capable of awesome design cuts and markings on a large variety of materials and very easy to use.

The cricut machines have the capability to cut large number of materials accurately and quickly. The range of materials varies from the delicate paper to leather then to thicker materials such as wood. With the aid of powerful rotary blades, the machine glides and rolls over any fabrics effortlessly leaving smooth and accurate cut on the material.

Cricut machines, at the core, are really cool printers. Technically, they die cutters and creative planners that help you put together cool designs for various items that you want to make. There are a lot of models out there, and many great types to choose from.

The Explore series of machines contain software called Cricut Design Space, which allows for you to design in the space whatever you want to make, and then literally print it out.

If you're sick and tired of making the same images each time, or you're looking to cut out a design in vinyl without tearing your hair out, then a Cricut machine could really help you.

The Cricut is a die-cutting machine, which is also known as a craft plotter or a cutting machine. Its format allows you to do projects that range from simple to complex on a seemingly limitless number of materials. From thin metal sheets to fabric, you can bring your designs to life with this innovative craft machine.

Cricut has a massive base of users who are enthusiastic to share their projects, tutorials, tips for care, tricks for usage, and other materials that can be used with their Cricut Makers. The resources for a crafter using a Cricut machine are nearly limitless.

A Cricut machine has the capacity to cut materials ranging from paper to faux leather, just to mention a few. In case you don't have good handwriting, you can also use this machine to that effect. In other words, you can make a Cricut do the job of a printer for you.

This is possible loading a marker in the accessory slot of the machine. When you do this, you can then proceed by making the machine draw the design you desire. Hence, the Cricut

machine is also a multifaceted machine that is designed to bring some versatility to your table.

Designs written by loading the marker of the accessory slot of the Cricut machine are always exquisite. Interestingly, you don't have to even use physical cartridges with some versions of the Cricut machine! The Explore series is a typical example of such versions of Cricut machines.

These series of Cricut machines are designed such that you can use the online design software instead. What this implies is that any shape or text you desire can be selected from this platform. The specific design you want can then be sent to the machine in order for you to cut it out.

Interestingly, the Explore series of the Cricut machine also makes it possible for direct upload. Hence, you can simply upload the particular design you want and use the machine to cut it out.

In addition to this awesomeness, a digital sewing pattern library is stored in the cricut maker for the user to access hundreds of patterns from different brand names such as Riley Blake and Simplicity. You can pick a number of projects from the library and boom, the machine cuts every piece you desire.

The Cricut Design Space allows the user to access any one of the over 50 projects in its library including 25 digital sewing

patterns. Not only that, it also allows you to upload an image to create a customized design of your own. The capabilities of the Cricut Maker Machine are just endless: Iron-on decorations on t-shirts, leather, vinyl decors, wood puzzles and sewing projects are some of the DIY or craft projects you can do using the machine.

The Cricut Design Space software can be operated with IOS or Android device having a USB charging.

How Does It Work?

When you see the finished product from a Cricut machine, you will definitely be blown away. The neatness and appealing look of a typical project done with the Cricut machine will take your breath away. However, only a few people understand the process involved in the creation of such amazing designs.

Have a Design

If you have a PC, you can access the Cricut Design Space to access the library of designs. If you have a Mac, you can access the same platform to select a huge variety of designs. In case you don't have any of these two but possesses an iPhone or

Chapter 2 Model Overview

Purchasing a Cricut Machine may not be very cheap, but choosing your model should mostly depend on your needs, and what you wish to do with these machines. If you have never used a Cricut machine before, then you will need to start with the easiest machine to operate. As a manufacturer of tools and accessories for DIY crafts, Cricut has several models that can serve all kinds of users. From all the Cricut Models, there are four which are most interesting: the ones from the Explore family (Cricut Explore One, Cricut Explore Air, and Cricut Explore Air 2), and of course, the Cricut Maker, which is the best Cricut Machine you can hope for.

Before you even start to think about the price of these models, it would be nice to understand what they can do.

Cricut Explore One

This machine is the most basic one you can get from the Explore family. Derived from its predecessor (Cricut Explore), this tool can be the perfect starter machine for you if you are not familiar with any of the Cricut products. Like most of the Cricut products, it's compatible with Design Space software (and allows you to upload your own images free of charge), can work with Cricut Cartridges, or can cut a pretty wide variety of materials. Plus, it comes with Smart Set Dial, a function you can use to easily configure the settings for each material.

If you just want to start your own small business, and have something pretty interesting in mind but you don't want to invest too much, for now, the Cricut Explore One can be the perfect choice for you. It can be bought for less than $200 on the Cricut website, Amazon, or other retailers. When you have great project ideas, then the sky is the limit when it comes to how much money you can make from your Cricut projects, so spending this amount can be considered a minor and very profitable investment on your part.

Cricut Explore Air

If you are looking for an amazing DIY value, look no further, as the Cricut Explore Air can be the perfect choice for you. In terms of features, this version is a bit more advanced than the original Cricut Explore. It includes the Smart Set Dial, a double tool holder for writing and one-click cutting, and it works with Design Space software (for Mac/iOS/Windows/Android). Obviously, you will be able to upload your own images free of charge, but the machine can also work with Cricut Cartridges and cut plenty of materials. When it comes to connectivity, Cricut Explore Air comes with a Bluetooth option for wireless cutting. This type of connectivity can be very handy in plenty of cases but bear in mind that it might fail if the projects you are trying to create are quite big.

The manufacturer, Amazon, or other retailers can offer great deals on this machine, so don't be shocked if you can find this product at a heavily discounted price. When you think of what it can do, it's definitely worth it to pay a discounted price for Cricut Explore Air.

Cricut Explore Air 2

If you are looking for the best product from the Explore Family, then you will need to try Cricut Explore Air 2. This machine is like an upgraded version of Explore Air, and it's known for its time-saving performance. It has more features than the older versions, and so far, it's been a very appreciated product by plenty of users. The biggest advantage of this version is that it comes with both Smart Set dial and Fast Mode. So you can easily go through material settings, plus you write and cut 2 times faster, hence its time-saving performance and increased productivity.

Plus, you will get all the existing features of the Explore Family products like:

- Bluetooth connectivity for wireless cutting

- Double tool holding for both writing and one-click cutting

- It allows you to upload your own images using the Design Space software

- It can cut plenty of materials

- It can work with Cricut Cartridges

Therefore, if you are looking for a powerful Cricut Machine that has plenty of features and can be a time-saver, then the Cricut Explore Air 2 is the perfect choice for you. When it comes to the price, this version is a bit more expensive compared to the older versions, but it totally worth the investment, especially when you buy this product at a discounted price, or with a bundle (this option may include different accessories).

Cricut Maker

Without any doubt, the premium or the flagship machine of Cricut is the Maker. If you are looking to expand your craft business, then this is the right tool for you. The Cricut Maker has plenty of features, as you can see below:

- it has Bluetooth connectivity included, for wireless cutting

- it comes with a double tool holder for writing and one-click cutting

- it allows you to upload your images for free using the Design Space software

- you can cut even more materials compared to the older versions

- it comes with Fast Mode included, so you can write or cut two times faster

- it has a special Rotary Blade for fabrics

- it includes a Knife Blade for thicker materials

- Simple and Double Scoring Wheel

- Adaptive Tool System, which is a feature for cutting hundreds of other materials

One of the best things with the Cricut machines is that you can select the color that you like the most, so it's not like you are limited to one color (white or black). Therefore, for the Explore version, you can select between Green and Wild Orchid. The Explore One comes with more color options: Blue, Pink Poppy, Navy Bloom, Coral, or Grey. You will get different color options with Explore Air: Gold, Teal, Wild Orchid, Poppy, and Blue. By far, the Explore Air 2 has the most options you can select from including White Pearl (Martha Stewart), Wisteria, Sunflower, Sky, Rose, Raspberry, Persimmon, Periwinkle, Peacock, Mint, Merlot, Lilac, Gold, Ivory (Anna Griffin), Fuschi, Denim, Coral, Cobalt, Cherry Blossom, Boysenberry, Blue, and Black.

The Cricut Maker only comes with three color options: Rose, Blue, and Champagne. Some colors may be exclusive to specific retailers, so these colors may not be found in the manufacturer's online store.

Choosing the Right Cricut for You

There are several aspects you will need to consider when selecting the right Cricut Machine for you, like:

- your experience with these kinds of machines

- your budget

- what projects you want to create

- what materials you want to cut

When you don't have too much experience with such machines, and you are definitely not familiar with any of the Cricut Machines, then it's wise to choose an entry-level machine from the Explore family. Perhaps this is why they included these machines in the Explore family, as it lets you explore the functions and features of a Cricut Machine. Any of these machines can be considered teasers of the Cricut Maker, which can be easily considered the ultimate cutting machine. If you are a beginner but want to quickly learn and implement some of your great ideas into projects, then the Cricut Explore Air 2 can be considered the perfect option for you. You can easily find a color you prefer, plus you will find all kinds of deals from the Cricut Shop or online retailers, offering you the product at a good price.

However, if you are very familiar with these machines, and you want to cut even thicker materials, then you really need to get the Cricut Maker, especially if you have some projects in mind that can help you make plenty of money. Regardless of the version you select, in most cases the prices are reasonable and you can easily recover your initial investment in such a machine.

Chapter 3 What Materials Can I Use

The capabilities of your Cricut Machine are influenced by the blades you are using (or can use with it). Depending on the blades you are using, you can cut more or fewer materials. Using the Cricut Explore Family machines you can cut plenty of materials, most of them with the Premium Fine-Point Blade. Of course, when cutting the materials, you need to modify the cut pressure, and if you are having issues cutting that specific material and increasing the pressure doesn't solve the issues, you may need to adjust the blade depth.

Therefore, with a Cricut Machine from the Explore Series, you can cut the following materials:

- paper (more or less thick)

- vinyl

- iron on

- light cardstock

- cardstock

- fabric

- poster board

- distressed craft foam

- plus craft foam

- craft foam

- adhesive-backed cork

- notebook paper

- wrapping paper

- aluminum foil

- washi sheet

- wax paper

- washi tape

- wax paper

- washi tape

- glitter vinyl

- printable iron-on

- patterned iron-on

- premium outdoor vinyl

- construction paper

- copy paper

- foil iron-on

- aluminum foil

- sticky note

- adhesive foil

- pearl paper

- premium vinyl

- printable vinyl

- stencil vinyl

- parchment paper

- cutting mat protector

- holographic vinyl

- neon iron-on

- SportFlex iron-on

- Mulberry foil paper

- duct tape sheet

- holographic sparkle vinyl

- window cling

- faux suede

- iron-on holographic sparkle

- felt

- sticker paper

- cardstock for intricate cuts

- matte adhesive foil

- grocery bag

- clear printable sticker paper

- chalkboard vinyl

- printable fabric

- flocked paper

- shimmer leather (1 mm)

- glitter iron-on

- genuine leather

- adhesive-backed magnetic sheet

- non-adhesive vinyl (16 gauge)

- paint chip

- heavy patterned paper

- vellum

- kraft cardstock

- foil paper (0.36 mm)

- canvas

- bonded oil cloth*

- bonded silk*

- photo paper

- bonded polyester*

- kraft board

- metallic leather

- foil acetate

- medium cardstock (80 lb)

- poster board

- metallic poster board

- light patterned paper

- faux leather (paper-thin)

- foil poster board

- Mulberry Epoxy paper

- birch

- Deluxe printer paper (0.23 mm)

- flat cardboard

- transparency

- sparkle paper

- shimmer paper

- tattoo paper

- corrugated cardboard

- party foil

- embossed foil paper

- bonded denim*

- magnetic sheet (0.5 mm)

- magnetic sheet (0.6 mm)

- light chipboard (0.55 mm)

- Epoxy Glitter paper

- heavy watercolor paper (140 lb)

- aluminum (0.14 mm)

- glitter cardstock

- wool fabric felt

- wool bonded felt*

- light glitter paper

- stencil film (0.4 mm)

- bonded burlap*

If you check the list above, you will see that some of the materials have the symbol "*" next to them. These materials need stabilizers to be cut properly. Most of the materials can be cut using the Premium Fine-Point Blade, but there other materials that require Deep-Point Blade (foam/aluminum foil), or the Bonded Fabric Blade (for fabrics, obviously). Each material has a different cut pressure, so when you are cutting these materials you need to check for this setting first. Therefore, use the pressure dial to set the right pressure on the machine, but remember about the Smart Set Dial, as you can easily set the material settings with the most basic materials. However, when you need to cut a material which is not shown on the Smart Set Dial, you can just select Custom and put the right pressure for the material.

With the Cricut Maker, you can cut all the materials mentioned above, plus a lot more, as you can see below:

- Garment leather (2-3 oz)

- Tooling leather (2-3 oz)

- Garment leather (4-5 oz)

- Tooling leather (4-5 oz)

- Tooling leather (6-7 oz)

- Acetate

- Adhesive foil

- Matte adhesive foil

- Aluminum foil

- Balsa wood - 1/16"

- Balsa wood - 3/32"

- Bamboo fabric

- Basswood - 1/16"

- Basswood - 1/32"

- Bengaline

- Permanent adhesive birch

- Boucle

- Broadcloth

- Burlap

- Burn-out velvet

- Calico

- Cambric

- Canvas

- Carbon fiber

- Cardstock (for more intricate cuts)

- Adhesive-backed cardstock

- Cashmere

- Cereal box

- Chalkboard vinyl

- Challis

- Chambray

- Chantilly lace

- Charmeuse Satin

- Chiffon

- Chintz

- Clear Printable Sticker Paper

- Colored duct tape

- Copy paper - 20 lb

- Corduroy

- Corrugated cardboard

- Cotton

- Bonded cotton

- Craft foam

- Crepe Charmeuse

- Crepe de Chine

- Crepe Paper

- Crepe-back satin

- Cutting mat protector

- Damask

- Delicate fabrics (like Tulle)

- Deluxe paper

- Denim

- Bonded denim

- Dotted Swiss

- Double Cloth

- Double Knit

- Dry Erase Vinyl

- Duck Cloth

- Duct Tape Sheet

- Dupioni Silk

- Embossed Foil Paper

- EVA Foam

- Extra Heavy Fabrics (e.g. Burlap)

- Eyelet

- Faille

- Faux Fur

- Faux Leather (Paper Thin)

- Faux Suede

- Felt

- AcryliC Fabric Felt

- Craft Bonded Felt

- Glitter Bonded Felt

- Stiff Felt

- Wool Bonded Felt

- Wool Fabric Felt

- Flannel

- Flat Cardboard

- Fleece

- Flex Foam

- Flocked Iron-on

- Flocked Paper

- Foil Acetate

- Foil Iron-On

- Foil Paper (0.36 mm)

- Foil Poster Board

- Foulard

- Freezer Paper

- Fusible Fleece

- Fusible Interfacing

- Gabardine

- Gauze

- Gel Sheet

- Genuine Leather

- Georgette

- Glitter Cardstock

- Glitter Craft Foam

- Glitter Duct Tape

- Glitter Iron-On

- Glitter Vinyl

- Gossamer

- Grocery Bag

- Grois Point

- Grosgrain

- Habutai

- Handmade Paper

- Heat Transfer

- Heather

- Heavy Chipboard 2.0 mm

- Heavy Fabrics (e.g. denim)

- Bonded Heavy Fabrics (e.g. denim)

- Heavy Patterned Paper

- Heavy Watercolor Paper - 140 lb

- Holographic Cardstock

- Holographic Heat Transfer

- Holographic Sparkle Vinyl

- Holographic Vinyl

- Homespun Fabric

- Insulbrite Batting

- Interlock Knit

- Iron-On

- Holographic Sparkle Iron-On - 0.1 mm

- Jacquard

- Jersey

- Jute

- Kevlar

- Khaki

- Kraft Board

- Kraft Cardstock

- Cardstock (for intricate cuts)

- La Coste

- Lame

- Light Cardstock - 60 lb

- Light Chipboard (0.37 mm)

- Light Cotton

- Light Fabrics (e.g. silk)

- Bonded Light Fabrics (e.g. Silk)

- Light Patterned Paper

- Linen

- Bonded Linen

- Lycra

- Magnetic Sheet (0.5 mm)

- Magnetic Sheet (0.6 mm)

- Matboard 4 Ply

- Matelasse

- Matte Vinyl

- Medium Cardstock - 80 lb

- Medium Fabrics (e.g. Cotton)

- Bonded Medium Fabrics (e.g. Cotton)

- Melton Wool

- Mesh

- Metal (40 gauge thin)

- Metallic Leather

- Metallic Leather

- Metallic Poster Board

- Metallic Vinyl

- Microfiber

- Moiree

- Moleskin

- Monk's Cloth

- Mulberry Foil Paper

- Mulberry Paper

- Muslin

- Neoprene

- Notebook Paper

- Nylon

- Bonded Oil Cloth

- Oil cloth

- Organza

- Ottoman

- Bonded Outdoor Vinyl

- Oxford

- Paint Chip

- Panne Velvet

- Adhesive-Backed Paper

- Party Foil

- Patterned Glitter Cardstock

- Patterned Iron-On

- Pearl Paper

- Peau de Soie

- Photo Paper

- Pima Cotton

- Pique Cotton

- Plastic Canvas

- Plastic Packaging

- Plisse

- Plush

- Bonded Polyester

- Poplin

- Poster Board

- Premium Outdoor Vinyl

- Premium Vinyl

- Printable Fabric

- Printable Foil

- Dark Printable Iron-On

- Light Printable Iron-On

- Printable Magnetic Sheet

- Quilt Batting

- Ramie

- Raschel Knit

- Rayon Lyocell

- Rib Knit

- Rice Paper

- Rip-Stop Nylon

- Sailcloth

- Sandblast Stencil

- Satin Silk

- Seesucker

- Sequined

- Shantung

- Shantung Santeen

- Shimmer Leather - 1 mm

- Shimmer Paper

- Silk China

- Bonded Silk

- Slinky Knit

- Spandex

- Sparkle Paper

- SportFlex Iron-On

- Stencil Film 0.4 mm

- Stencil Vinyl

- Sticker Paper

- Sticker Paper Removable

- Sticky Note

- Suede

- Taffeta

- Tattoo Paper

- Terry Cloth

- Tissue Paper

- Transfer Foil

- Transfer Sheet

- Transparency

- Tulle

- Tweed

- Ultra Firm Stabilizer

- Vellum

- Velour

- Velvet Upholstery

- Velveteen

- Vinyl

- Viscose

- Voile

- Waffle Cloth

- Washi Sheet

- Wax Paper

- Window Cling

- Wool Crepe

- Wrapping Paper

- Ziberline

The Smart Set Dial doesn't appear on Cricut Maker, but this machine uses something else instead. The Adaptive Tool System is used to cut so many materials for this model.

.

Chapter 4 Machine Add-On's, Tools and Cricut Access

Tools

There are a variety of tools that can be purchased to compliment the Cricut. No matter the model that fits your lifestyle. Thankfully Cricut has compiled most of the essential tools into convenient sets. Either to start off first-time Cricut users with the necessities or for special projects, like crafting and sewing.

If purchasing a toolset is not the path you wish to take, the tools can be bought separately. In addition, there are other tools that can be bought that are not in a kit. Below is a list of kits and tools with a short explanation of their various purposes.

Tool Kits

Basic Tool Kit

All the 5 essential tools in one package;

- Scraper to clean and polish

- Spatula to lift

- Micro-tip scissors

- Weeder for vinyl

- Tweezers

Basics Starter Tool Kit

Another set of essential tools including;

- Scraper and spatula

- Point pens in metallic

- Scoring stylus

- Deep Cut Housing and 1 blade

Essential Tool Kit

Made for Cricut Explore models, this 7-piece set includes;

- Trimmer and replacement blade

- Scoring stylus

- Scraper for cleaning and polishing

- Spatula

- Micro-blade scissors

- Weeder

- Tweezers

Paper Crafting Tool Kit

This 4-piece set is perfect for professional paper crafting and includes;

- Craft mat

- Distresser for edges

- Quilling tool for spirals

- Piercer for small piece placement

Sewing Tool Kit

Sewing essentials are all in one place. This set includes;

- **Thimble made of leather**

- **Measuring tape**

- **Pins and pin cushion**

- **Seam ripper**

- **Thread snips**

- **Fabric shears**

Weeding Tool Kit

A set of 5 tools for elaborate cutting and vinyl DIY crafts includes;

- Hook tweezers

- Fine tweezers

- Hook weeder

- Weeder

- Piercer

Complete Starter Tool Kit

Perfect for the beginning Cricut user, this set includes;

- Black window cling

- Cutting mat

- Point pens in metallic

- Scoring stylus

- Deep Cut Housing and 1 Blade

- Scraper to clean and polish

- Spatula to lift

- Micro-tip scissors

- Weeder to remove negatives

- Tweezers

Single Tools

XL Scraper

Clean mats quickly and easily or adhere sizeable projects to an assortment of surfaces with this tool. Great for vinyl and can be used with all Circuit models.

Portable Trimmer

Precision cutting is achieved with the 12-inch swinging arm, and the storage for a replacement blade makes this an extra-functional tool. Swiftly insert materials, cut, and measure from both directions with the dual-hinged rails.

Scoring Stylus

3-dimensional projects, boxes, card, and envelopes' lines can be scored in 1 step with this tool that holds the blade for cutting and the stylus. This tool is best for Cricut Maker and Explorer models.

Applicator and Remover

Remove or apply textiles easily and make the cutting mat last longer with these functional tools. Ideal for the Cricut Maker, these tools are sold together to make working with fabric that much easier (applicator is also known as a brayer).

Scraper and Spatula

Lift and clean easily with these two tools. Made especially for the cutting mat for all sorts of projects.

Scissors

Make clean cuts with micro-tip scissors, and store them safely with the included end cap and cover for the blades (you can use a medical scissor too).

Tweezers

Secure project pieces after lifting them with the reverse-grip of this tool. Perfect to use for little items like small cuts and intricate trimmings.

Weeders

Use this tool to remove small cuts and for separating iron-on pieces and vinyl from their liners.

Accessories

Similar to the tools available for the Cricut, there are also a variety of accessories that can be purchased to compliment whatever model of

Cricut you choose. Below is a list that highlights some of the available accessories and their functions. Consider purchasing them individually or take advantage of the different bundles and sets offered.

Functional Support Accessories

Specially designed accessories are made to enhance the experience of using a Cricut machine with function and style.

Mats

- Light grip

- Standard grip

- Strong grip

- Fabric grip

Scoring and Blades

- Rotary blade

- Fabric blade- bonded

- Deep cut blade

- Fine-point blade

- Premium blade made of German carbide

- Scoring stylus

Pens

- Variety of colored pens

- Extra fine tip colored pens

- Ultimate fine tip colored pens

- Fabric pen that is washable

- Variety of colored markers

Tape

- Glitter tape

Adapters and Tech

- Cartridge adapter

- Pen adapter

- Bluetooth adapter

- Accessory adapter

- USB cable

- Power cord

- Keyboard overlay

For the crafter on the go or in need of stylish and functional storage, these accessories are the perfect fit.

Pouches

- Accessory pouches for tools

Totes and Bags

- Crafters shoulder bag

- Rolling crafters tote

- Machine tote

Machine Add-On's

Cricut machines can accomplish many great things, but sometimes they could use a sidekick. That's where these machines come in.

Easy Press

Achieve the iron-on results like a professional in less than a minute! Simple to use and light to carry, this accessory is the perfect for Cricut users who want t-shirt transfers to last.

Easy Press Bundles:

- Bulk

- Ultimate

- Everything

Cuttlebug

Cut or emboss almost any material on the run with this handy machine. Achieve the professional, clean cuts you want with ease.

Cuttlebug Add-on's:

- Mats

- Dies

- Materials

- Spacer plates

- Cutting mats

Bright Pad

This durable, light pad offers a soft, adjustable light to make tracing, cutting, and easier and more comfortable on the eyes.

Sets

Basic

Perfect for the Explore machines, this set includes spatula and scraper tools, a pen set, a stylus for scoring, and a deep cut blade with its housing.

Ultimate

An enhanced set of accessories for the Explore machines, this set includes black window cling, 3 different cutting mats, a pen set, a stylus for scoring, and a deep cut blade and its housing. It also includes the basic toolset which contains spatula and scraper tools, scissors with a blade cover, a weeder, and tweezers.

Cricut Access

To maximize the possibilities with the different machines, Cricut offers a service called "Access." This membership has different levels and unique benefits such as discounts and member-only access to design services. Three different Access memberships are listed below with a brief explanation of each one.

Fonts

Hundreds of fonts, some that non-members cannot access, are available in the most affordable Access membership, Fonts. It costs $5 per month. It's not a contract, meaning at any time you can cancel the membership.

Limitations include that they are only to be used with Explore and Maker machines and the fonts do not include licensed fonts, like Disney.

Standard

A more comprehensive Access membership; Standard, offers more exclusive access and benefits. Any purchase on Cricut.com and Design Space is 10% off, and the database includes over 30,000 images, many of which are not available for non-members. It also includes the same benefits as Fonts, including the ability to cancel when needed. The cost for this membership is about $8 per month.

The limitation of this membership is that it does not include many licensed cartridges, fonts, or images such as Disney, Sesame, or Sanrio Hello Kitty products. This is probably a good package to go with if you are starting out.

Premium

The most comprehensive Access membership; Premium, combines the benefits of Fonts and Standard memberships and adds on more. Additional cartridges, images, and fonts are up to 50% off in Design Space. Free shipping is also offered for orders with a total over $50. For a yearly fee of about $120 ($10 a month), it includes access to over 1,000 projects.

One limitation, like the other memberships, is that Premium does not have access to many licensed cartridges, images, and fonts and the

50% discount cannot be applied to purchase of these items. The discounts cannot be used with other promotional offers.

Cartridges

This unique feature of the Cricut allows anyone access to professional images and fonts for whatever they desire to create. Professional to novice crafters can enjoy the versatility of the cartridges easily. The range of cartridges offered fit just about any need you may have, and one cartridge offers a variety of ideas within its theme. Simply insert the cartridge into your machine and link it to your Cricut account online to use the images and fonts. Create the perfect designs for whatever occasion! You can order cartridges online too.

Some of the cartridges available are listed below.

Licensed characters and themes

- Disney

- Sanrio

- Boy Scouts

- Marvel

- Wordsworth

- Teresa Collins

Specially designed for cards

- Holiday, Birthday and Thank you cards

- Special card designs such as pop-up designs, box cards, and everyday themes

Events

- **Weddings**

- **Birthdays**

- **Babies**

- **Graduations**

- **Anniversaries**

Seasons

- Spring

- Summer

- Fall

- Winter

Holidays

- Christmas

- Hanukkah

- Easter

- Thanksgiving

- New Year's

- Mother's and Father's Day

Perfect for every day

- Home décor images and fonts

- Sports images and fonts

- Religious images and fonts

- Children related images and fonts such as animals, school, and toys

Special fonts

- Disney fonts

- Varsity fonts

- Holiday-themed fonts

- Themed fonts

- Non-English fonts such as American Sign Language, the Greek alphabet, and Hebrew

Chapter 5 Paper-Based Projects

I t is ideal to start your first project using paper-based designs, since these projects are easier to not only design but also to cut, regardless of the kind of "Cricut" cutting machine being used. You can get professional-looking results without investing a whole lot of time and money. You will learn to create a variety of projects that you can further customize as you follow the instructions below and have unique designs of your own.

Recipe Stickers

Materials needed – "Cricut" cutting machine, sticker paper, and cutting mat.

Step 1

Use your "Cricut ID" to log in to the "Design Space" application. Then click on the "New Project" button on the top right corner of the screen to start a new project and view a blank canvas.

Step 2

Click on the "Images" icon on the "Design Panel" and type in "recipe stickers" in the search bar. Select the image that works for you, then click on the "Insert Images" button at the bottom of the screen, as shown in the picture below.

Step 3

The image that you have selected will appear on the canvas and can be edited to your preference. You will be able to make all kinds of changes, for example, changing the color and size of the image (sticker should be between 2-4 inches wide). The image selected for this project has the words "stickers" inside the design, so let's delete that by first clicking on the "Ungroup" button and selecting the "Stickers" layer and clicking on the red "x" button. Click on the "Text" button and add the name of your recipe, as shown in the picture below.

Step 4

Now, move the text to the middle of the design and select the entire design, including the text. Then click on "Align" and select "Center Horizontally" and "Center Vertically" so that your text will be uniformly aligned right in the center of the design.

Step 5

Select all the layers of the design and click on the "Group" icon on the top right of the screen under "Layers Panel." Now, copy and paste the designs and update the text for all your recipes, as shown in the picture below. (Tip – You can use your keyboard shortcuts like "Ctrl + C" (to copy) and "Ctrl + V" (to paste) instead of selecting the image and clicking on "Edit" from the "Edit bar" to view the dropdown option for "Copy" and "Paste".)

Step 6

Click on "Save" at the top right corner of the screen and enter a name for your project, for example, "Recipe Stickers," then click "Save," as shown in the picture below.

Step 7

Your design is ready to be cut. Simply click on the "Make It" button on the top right corner of the screen. All the required mats and materials will be displayed on the screen. (Tip: You can move your design on the mat by simply dragging and dropping it anywhere on the mat to resemble the cutting space for your material on the actual cutting mat).

Step 8

Once you have loaded the sticker paper to your "Cricut" cutting machine, click "Continue" at the bottom right corner of the screen to start cutting your design.

Step 9

Once your "Cricut" device has been connected to your computer, set the cut setting to "Vinyl" (recommended to cut the sticker paper since it tends to be thicker than regular paper). Place the sticker paper on top of the cutting mat and load it into the "Cricut" device by pushing it against the rollers. The "Load/Unload" button would already be flashing, so just press that button first, followed by the flashing "Go" button. Viola! You have just created your very own recipe stickers.

Wedding Invitations

Materials needed – "Cricut" cutting machine, cutting mat, and cardstock or your choice of decorative paper/crepe paper/fabric, home printer (if not using "Cricut Maker").

Step 1

Use your "Cricut ID" to log in to the "Design Space" application. Then click on the "New Project" button on the top right corner of the screen to start a new project and view a blank canvas.

Step 2

A beginner-friendly way to create wedding invitations is a customization of an already existing project form the "Design Space" library that aligns with your own ideas. Click on the "Projects" icon on the "Design Panel" then select "Cards" from the "All Categories" drop-down. Enter the

Step 3

You can click on the project to preview its description and requirements. Once you have found the project you want to use, click "Customize" at the bottom of the screen, so you can edit the invite and add the required text to it.

Step 4

The design will be loaded on to the canvas. Click on the "Text" button and type in the details for your invite. You will be able to modify the font, color as well as the alignment of the text from the "Edit Text Bar" on top of the screen. You can even adjust the size of the entire design as needed. (An invitation card can be anywhere from 6 to 9 inches wide)

Step 5

Select the entire design and click on the "Group" icon on the top right of the screen under "Layers Panel." Then click on the "Save" button to enter a name for your project and click "Save" again.

Step 6

Your design can now be printed then cut. Simply click on the "Make It" button on the top right corner of the screen to view the required mats and material. Then use your home printer to print the design on your chosen material (white cardstock or paper), or if using the "Cricut Maker," then just follow the prompts on the "Design Space" application.

Step 7

Load the material with printed design to your "Cricut" cutting machine and click "Continue" at the bottom right corner of the screen to start cutting your design.

Step 8

Once your "Cricut" device has been connected to your computer, set the cut setting to "cardstock." Then place the printed cardstock on top of the cutting mat and load into the "Cricut" device by pushing against the rollers. The "Load/Unload" button would already be flashing, so just press that button first, followed by the flashing "Go" button. Viola! You have your wedding invitations all ready to be put in an envelope and on their way to all your wedding guests.

Custom Notebooks

Materials needed – "Cricut" cutting machine, cutting mat, and washi sheets or your choice of decorative paper/crepe paper/fabric.

Step 1

Use your "Cricut ID" to log in to the "Design Space" application. Then click on the "New Project" button on the top right corner of the screen to start a new project and view a blank canvas.

Step 2

Let's use an already existing project from the "Cricut" library for this. Click on the "Projects" icon on the "Design Panel" and type in "notebook" in the search bar.

You can view all the projects available by clicking on them, and a pop-up window displaying all the details of the project will appear on your screen.

Step 3

Select the project that you like and click on "Customize," so you can further edit this project to your preference.

Step 4

The selected project will be displayed on the Canvas. You can check from the "Layers Panel" if your design contains only one layer, which is very easy to modify or multiple layers that can be selectively modified. Click on the "Linetype Swatch" to view the color palette and select the desired color for your design.

Step 5

Once you have modified the design to your satisfaction, it is ready to be cut. Simply click on the "Make It" button on the top right corner of the screen to view the required mats and material for your project.

Step 6

Load the washi paper sheet to your "Cricut" cutting machine and click "Continue" at the bottom right corner of the screen to start cutting your design.

Step 7

Connect your "Cricut" device to your computer and place the washi paper or your chosen paper on top of the cutting mat and load into the "Cricut" machine by pushing against the rollers. The "Load/Unload" button would already be flashing, so just press that button first, followed by the flashing "Go" button. Viola! Your kids can now enjoy their uniquely customized notebook.

Paper Flowers

Materials needed – "Cricut" cutting machine, cutting mat, cardstock, and adhesive.

Step 1

Use your "Cricut ID" to log in to the "Design Space" application. Then click on the "New Project" button on the top right corner of the screen to start a new project and view a blank canvas.

Step 2

Click on the "Images" icon on the "Design Panel" and type in "flower" in the search bar. Then select the image that you like and click on the "Insert Images" button at the bottom of the screen.

Step 3

The selected image will be displayed on the canvas and can be edited using applicable tools from the "Edit Image Bar." Then copy and paste the flower five times and make them a size smaller than the preceding flower to create a variable size for depth and texture for the design. Click on the "Linetype Swatch" to view the color palette and select the desired color for your design.

Step 5

Once you have modified the design to your satisfaction, it is ready to be cut. Simply click on the "Make It" button on the top right corner of the screen to view the required mats and material for your project.

Step 6

Load the cardstock to your "Cricut" cutting machine and click "Continue" at the bottom right corner of the screen to start cutting your design.

Step 7

Connect your "Cricut" device to your computer and place the cardstock or your chosen paper on top of the cutting mat and load into the "Cricut" machine by pushing against the rollers. The "Load/Unload" button would already be flashing, so just press that button first, followed by the flashing "Go" button.

Step 8

Once the design has been cut, simply remove the cut flowers and bend them at the center. Then using the adhesive, stack the flowers with the largest flower at the bottom.

Chapter 6 Easy Cricut Projects

Project 1 - "Queen B" T-shirt

Project Tools, Materials, and Accessories:

- Plain cotton T-shirt in the color of your choice

- Iron-on vinyl, also called heat transfer vinyl (HTV) — gold

- Green StandardGrip mat

- Cricut Fine-Point Blade

- Weeding tool

- Pair of scissors for cutting the material to size

- Brayer

- Iron or the Cricut EasyPress Iron

- Cricut heat press mat to iron on

Directions:

1. Start a new project in Design Space.

2. Choose 'Templates' from the left-hand side menu.

3. Choose the 'Classic T-shirts' template.

4. From the top menu, choose the type of T-shirt — kids short sleeve.

5. From the top menu, choose the size of the T-shirt — small.

6. The back and the front of the T-shirt will appear on Design Space in the workspace.

7. From the top menu, select the color of the T-shirt you are using — pink.

8. Select 'Text' from the left-hand menu and type in "Queen B."

9. Set the font; a great free font for this project is Bauhaus 93.

10. Position the text on the T-shirt, then set the size and change the color to gold.

11. Choose images and find a bee picture. There is a nice free image or some really cute images you can buy.

12. Position the bee above the B and set the color to gold. You can rotate it into a tilted position.

13. Click on the 'Make it' button, and you will be prompted with another screen showing the design on the cutting board. This is because, for iron-on vinyl, you need to mirror the image. You mirror the image in order to iron it on with the correct side up. Click the 'Mirror' button on the left-hand side of the screen. You will see your writing and image look like it is back-to-front.

14. Reset your dial on the Cricut to custom.

15. In Design Space, choose the everyday iron-on for your material setting.

16. You can set the pressure to a bit more if you like.

17. You will see a warning letting you know that mirroring must be on for iron-on vinyl. It reminds you to place the vinyl facedown as well.

18. Check that you have the fine-point blade loaded in cartridge two of the Cricut. Nothing is needed for cartridge one.

19. Cut the vinyl to the space that is indicated by the Cricut Design Space.

20. Place the shiny side of the iron-on vinyl down onto the cutting mat. Use your brayer to smooth out the vinyl onto your mat.

21. Load the cutting into the Cricut, and when the Cricut is ready, click 'Go' for it to cut.

22. Unload the cutting mat when it has been cut. Remove the design from the mat, and gently remove the mat side of the vinyl from the carrier sheet (matte side of the vinyl).

23. Use the weeding tool to pick out the areas of the letters like the middles of the B.

24. Place your T-shirt onto the Cricut pressing mat with the middle section where you want the transfer to be.

25. If you are using the Cricut EasyPress, you can go to the Cricut website to find the heat transfer guide and the settings you will need for the press. Follow the instructions with the Cricut EasyPress.

26. For a normal iron, preheat the iron.

27. Place the Cricut heat press mat inside the shirt.

28. Heat the surface of the T-shirt for 15 seconds with the iron.

29. Put the design on the shirt where it is to be ironed on with the carrier sheet up.

30. Place a parchment sheet over the vinyl to protect the iron and the design.

31. Place the iron on the design and hold the iron in place on the design applying a bit of pressure for up to 3o seconds.

32. Turn the shirt inside out and place the iron on the back of the design for another 30 seconds.

33. When it is done, turn the shirt right side out and gently pull the carrier sheet off.

Project 2 - Car Keys, Wood Keyring

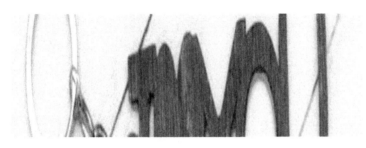

Project Tools, Materials, and Accessories:

- Wooden tags (L = 3.15" x W = 1.57" x D = 0.11")

- 1 medium-sized jump ring hoop (gold)

- 1 keyring hoop (gold)

- 1 4" to 5" gold link chain

- Green StandardGrip mat

- Cricut adhesive vinyl (color of your choice)

- Cricut transfer tape

- Cricut Fine-Point Blade

- Weeding tool

- Spatula

- Brayer or scraping tool

- Pair of scissors for cutting the material to size

Directions:

1. Open a new project in Design Space.

2. Choose 'Square' from the 'Shapes' menu.

3. Unlock the shape and size it to the length and width of the wooden key tag.

4. Position the rectangle at the top corner of the screen, leaving some bleeding room for the Cricut.

5. Find a cute picture of a car or search for one after choosing 'Images' from the left-hand window.

6. Unlock the image and scale it to the size you want it to be. For instance, if you want to position it at the bottom right corner of the wooden tag, you would need to make it a suitable size to fit that corner.

7. Choose 'Text' from the left-hand menu and type "Car Keys."

8. Select the font that you like and set it to the same color as the image.

9. Unlock the font, position it where you want it to sit on the keyring, then resize it to fit perfectly.

10. You might want to rotate the text so it runs long ways on the keyring.

11. Select the rectangle and delete it.

12. Select the image and the text, then click 'Attach' from the bottom right-hand menu (or right-click).

13. As you should not waste any pieces of vinyl, you can do a few of these keyring signs at a time.

14. From the 'Shapes' menu, select the 'Square' and unlock the shape.

15. Set the shape size to 12" by 12" and set the 'Fill' color to a light grey.

16. Click on the 'Arrange' top menu item and send the grey box to the back.

17. Move the Car Keys design onto the board position in the top left-hand corner of the grey box. Do not put it to close the edge, and leave some bleeding room for the Cricut and for you to cut the sign out.

18. Duplicate the design as many times as you need to. You can fit approximately 10 signs across and 3 signs down. If you do not want to leave any space, shrink the last row of keyring designs down to fit to make 4 rows of 10.

19. In order to edit each design's text, select each individually, hit 'Detach,' and double click on the text. Do not forget to 'Attach' once you have the correct text.

20. You will need to 'Flatten' each of the designs so that the text and car are cut out together.

21. When you have all the keyring signs laid out, select the grey backing square and delete it.

22. Select all the designs and 'Attach' to ensure they are printed on the same sheet of vinyl.

23. Stick the vinyl onto the cutting board, using the brayer or cutting tool to smooth it out.

24. Load the cutting board into the Cricut.

25. In Design Space, click 'Make it.'

26. Select the correct material and ensure the correct blade is loaded.

27. When the Cricut is ready, press 'Go.'

28. When the labels have been cut, use a pair of scissors to cut the design off the vinyl sheet.

29. Pull the top sheet off the design carefully and use the spatula if necessary.

30. Use the weeding tool to neaten up the design.

31. Place the transfer tape over the design, pull off the backing tape, and place it onto the wooden tag.

32. Use the scraping tool or your finger to make sure the vinyl has been stuck down properly onto the tag.

33. Gently pull off the transfer tape.

34. Connect the gold link chain to the jump ring on one end and the keyring loop to the other.

Project 3 - "Momma Bear on Board Keep Your Distance" Car Window Stickers

Project Tools, Materials, and Accessories:

- Outdoor glossy vinyl (clear or white)

- Green StandardGrip mat

- Cricut measuring tape

- Inkjet printer

- Transfer tape

- Rubbing alcohol

- Cricut Fine-Point Blade

- Weeding tool

- Spatula

- Brayer or scraping tool

- Pair of scissors for cutting the material to size

Directions:

1. Measure how big you are going to want the decal to be.

2. Open a new Design Space project.

3. Select 'Images' from the left-hand menu.

4. Type in "bear" in the search bar and choose the black bear (Image #MF7274E7).

5. Position it on the screen and scale it to the desired size.

6. Change the color of the bear to brown.

7. Select 'Text' from the left-hand menu, and reset the font to Bernard MT Condensed. It is a nice clear font with a bit of character.

8. Type "Momma Bear on Board" on the one line.

9. Hit enter and type "Keep Your Distance" on the next line.

10. Center the text and change the color to white.

11. Unlock the text and scale it to size, then position it in the center of the bear.

12. Make sure none of the letters hang over the side of the bear image.

13. Select both the bear image and text, then click 'Flatten' from the bottom right-hand menu. You can also right-click and choose 'Flatten.'

14. Save the project.

15. Click on 'Make it.'

16. Make sure the image is aligned correctly on the page and everything is the way you want it to be.

17. Click 'Continue.'

18. Load your outdoor glossy vinyl sheet into your Inkjet printer. When you are ready, click 'Send To Printer.'

19. Press 'Print' if you are happy with the print setup.

20. Once the printer has finished printing the decal, unload the vinyl sheet from the Inkjet printer.

21. Stick the printed decal onto the cutting mat.

22. Go back to your project in Design Space and choose the correct material.

23. Load the cutting mat into the Cricut, and when it is ready, press 'Go.'

24. When it is done, use the spatula, if necessary, to pull off the backing sheet of the vinyl.

25. Use the weeding tool to weed off any pieces that should not be there.

26. Cut some transfer paper to the size of the decal.

27. Place it over the decal. It is easier to work with it if it is stuck to the cutting mat.

28. Use the brayer or scraping tool to smooth the transfer tape over the image and get all the bubbles out.

29. Pull it off the cutting mat.

30. Take the rubbing alcohol and clean the portion of the car window that you want to place the decal on.

31. Gently pull the back of the vinyl off and position the decal on the cleaned window.

32. Once it is on the window, use the brayer or scraping tool to smooth it out and ensure it is properly stuck down.

Chapter 7 Cricut Projects with Vinyl

Project 1 - Perpetual Calendar

Woodblock calendars are a cute addition to any décor. Many teachers use them on their desks, or they fit in anywhere in your home. You can find unfinished block calendars online or at most craft stores. They'll usually have two wooden cubes for the numbers, two longer blocks for the months, and a stand to hold them. Painting the wood will give you the color of your choice, but you could also stain it or look around for calendars made of different types of wood. You can use the Cricut Explore One, Cricut Explore Air 2, or Cricut Maker for this project.

Supplies Needed

- Unfinished woodblock calendar

- Acrylic paint in color(s) of your choosing.

- Vinyl color(s) of your choosing

- Vinyl transfer tape

- Cutting mat

- Weeding tool or pick

- Mod Podge

Directions:

1. Paint the woodblock calendar in the colors you'd like and set aside to dry.

2. Open Cricut Design Space, and create a new project.

3. Create a square the correct size for the four blocks.

4. Select the "Text" button in the lower left-hand corner.

5. Choose your favorite font, and type the following numbers as well as all of the months: 0, 0, 1, 1, 2, 2, 3, 4, 5, 6, 7, 8

6. Place your vinyl on the cutting mat.

7. Send the design to your Cricut.

8. Use a weeding tool or pick to remove the excess vinyl from the text.

9. Apply transfer tape to each separate number and the months.

10. Remove the paper backing from the tape, and apply the numbers as follows.

   a. 0 and 5 on the top and bottom of the first block

   b. 1, 2, 3, 4 around the sides of the first block

   c. 0 and 8 on the top and bottom of the second block

   d. 1, 2, 6, 7 around the sides of the second block

11. Remove the paper backing from the tape on the months, and apply them to the long blocks, the first six months on one and the second six months on the other.

12. Rub the tape to transfer the vinyl to the wood, making sure there are no bubbles. Carefully peel the tape away.

13. Seal everything with a coat of Mod Podge.

14. Arrange your calendar to display today's date, and enjoy it year after year!

Project 2 - Wooden Gift Tags

Dress up your gifts with special wooden tags! Balsa wood is light and easy to cut. The wood tags with gold names will give all of your gifts a shabby chic charm. Change up the color of the vinyl as you see fit; you can even use different colors for different gift recipients. People will be able to keep these tags and use them for something else, as well. An alternative to balsa wood is chipboard, though it won't have the same look. The Cricut Maker is the best choice for this project, though the Cricut Explore One and Cricut Explore Air 2 can get by using the Deep Cut Blade.

Supplies Needed

- Balsa wood

- Gold vinyl

- Vinyl transfer tape

- Cutting mat

- Weeding tool or pick

Directions

1. Secure your small balsa wood pieces to the cutting mat, then tape the edges with masking tape for additional strength.

2. Open Cricut Design Space and create a new project.

3. Select the shape you would like for your tags and set the Cricut to cut wood, then send the design to the Cricut.

4. Remove your wood tags from the Cricut and remove any excess wood.

5. In Cricut Design Space, select the "Text" button in the lower left-hand corner.

6. Choose your favorite font, and type the names you want to place on your gift tags.

7. Place your vinyl on the cutting mat.

8. Send the design to your Cricut.

9. Use a weeding tool or pick to remove the excess vinyl from the text.

10. Apply transfer tape to the quote.

11. Remove the paper backing from the tape.

12. Place the names on the wood tags.

13. Rub the tape to transfer the vinyl to the wood, making sure there are no bubbles. Carefully peel the tape away.

14. Thread twine or string through the holes, and decorate your gifts!

Project 3 - Pet Mug

Show your love for your pet every morning when you have your coffee! A cute silhouette of a cat or dog with some paw prints is a simple but classy design. You're not limited to those two animals, either. Use a bird with bird footprints, a fish with water drops, or whatever pet you might have! You can add your pet's name or a quote to the design as well. You have the freedom here to arrange the aspects of the design however you'd like. You could put the animal in the center surrounded by the paw prints, scatter the prints all around the mug, place the animal next to its name and paw prints along the top, or whatever else you can imagine. Think of this as a tribute to your favorite pet or dedication to your favorite animal, and decorate accordingly. You can use the Cricut Explore One, Cricut Explore Air 2, or Cricut Maker for this project.

Supplies Needed

- Plain white mug
- Glitter vinyl
- Vinyl transfer tape
- Cutting mat
- Weeding tool or pick

Directions:

1. Open Cricut Design Space and create a new project.

2. Select the "Image" button in the lower left-hand corner and search for "cat," "dog," or any other pet of your choice.

3. Choose your favorite image and click "Insert."

4. Search images again for paw prints, and insert into your design.

5. Arrange the pet and paw prints how you'd like them on the mug.

6. Place your vinyl on the cutting mat.

7. Send the design to your Cricut.

8. Use a weeding tool or pick to remove the excess vinyl from the design.

9.   Apply transfer tape to the design.

10.   Remove the paper backing, and apply the design to the mug.

11.   Rub the tape to transfer the vinyl to the mug, making sure there are no bubbles. Carefully peel the tape away.

12.   Enjoy your custom pet mug!

Project 4 - Organized Toy Bins

How much of a mess is your kids' room? We already know the answer to that. Grab some plastic bins and label them with different toy categories, and teach your child to sort! You can use the type of bins that suit your child or their room best. Many people like to use the ones that look like giant buckets with handles on the sides. There are also more simple square ones. You could even use cheaper laundry baskets or plastic totes with or without the lids. Once your child is old enough to read the labels, it will be easier for them to put away toys and find them again to play. You can add images to the designs as well—whatever will make your child like them best! You can use the Cricut Explore One, Cricut Explore Air 2, or Cricut Maker for this project.

Supplies Needed

- Plastic toy bins in colors of your choice

- White vinyl

- Vinyl transfer tape

- Cutting mat

- Weeding tool or pick

Directions:

1. Open Cricut Design Space and create a new project.

2. Select the "Text" button in the lower left-hand corner.

3. Choose your favorite font and type the labels for each toy bin. See below for some possibilities.

   o Legos

   o Dolls

- o Cars

- o Stuffed animals

- o Outside Toys

4. Place your vinyl on the cutting mat.

5. Send the design to your Cricut.

6. Use a weeding tool or pick to remove the excess vinyl from the text.

7. Apply transfer tape to the words.

8. Remove the paper backing and apply the design to the bin.

9. Rub the tape to transfer the vinyl to the bin, making sure there are no bubbles. Carefully peel the tape away.

10. Organize your kid's toys in your new bins!

Project 5 - Froggy Rain Gear

Kids love to play outside in the rain. It can be hard to get them to dress properly for it, though. Decorate a raincoat and rain boots with a cute froggy design that will have them asking to wear them! A simple raincoat and boots that you can find at any store for a reasonable price become custom pieces with this project. The outdoor vinyl is made to withstand the elements and last for ages. You can customize this even more by adding your child's name or change up the theme completely with different images. You can use the Cricut Explore One, Cricut Explore Air 2, or Cricut Maker for this project.

Supplies Needed

- Matching green raincoat and rain boots

- White outdoor vinyl

- Vinyl transfer tape

- Cutting mat

- Weeding tool or pick

Directions:

1. Open Cricut Design Space and create a new project.

2. Select the "Image" button in the lower left-hand corner and search for "frog."

3. Choose your favorite frog and click "Insert."

4.   Copy the frog and resize. You will need three frogs, a larger one for the coat and two smaller ones for each boot.

5.   Place your vinyl on the cutting mat.

6.   Send the design to your Cricut.

7.   Use a weeding tool or pick to remove the excess vinyl from the design.

8.   Apply transfer tape to the design.

9.   Remove the paper backing and apply the design to the coat or boot.

10.   Rub the tape to transfer the vinyl to the rain gear, making sure there are no bubbles. Carefully peel the tape away.

11.   Dress your kid up to play in the rain!

Project 6 - Snowy Wreath

Wreaths are a popular decoration year-round. This one is perfect for winter. You can buy premade grapevine wreaths at almost any store, or you can get really crafty and assemble one yourself. The berry stems can be found in the floral sections of craft stores. Silver will fit the snowy theme well, but you could also use red for a holiday-themed look or an entirely different color. You can also change up the whole project to theme it toward your winter holiday of choice. You can use the Cricut Explore One, Cricut Explore Air 2, or Cricut Maker for this project.

Supplies Needed

- Grapevine wreath

- Silver berry stems

- Spray adhesive

- Silver and white glitter

- Piece of wood to fit across the center of the wreath

- Wood stain, if desired

- Drill and a small bit

- Twine

- White vinyl

- Vinyl transfer tape

- Cutting mat

- Weeding tool or pick

Directions:

1. Thread the silver berry stems throughout the grapevine wreath.

2. Use the spray adhesive and glitter to create patches of "snow" on the wreath.

3. If you want to stain your wood, do so now and set it aside to dry.

4. Open Cricut Design Space and create a new project.

5. Select the "Text" button in the lower left-hand corner.

6. Choose your favorite font and type, "Let it snow."

7. Place your vinyl on the cutting mat.

8. Send the design to your Cricut.

9. Use a weeding tool or pick to remove the excess vinyl from the text.

10. Apply transfer tape to the words.

11. Remove the paper backing and apply the design to the wood piece.

12. Rub the tape to transfer the vinyl to the wood, making sure there are no bubbles. Carefully peel the tape away.

13. Drill two small holes in the corner of the wood and thread the twine through.

14. Hang your wreath and sign for the winter season!

Chapter 8 Cricut Project with Synthetic Leather

Cactus Faux Leather Cricut Tote Bag!

Polka dot plants made from Cricut Creator, Iron on EasyPress and Cactus on faux leather tote bag! Is this bag not the perfect cactus tote?! It's easy to make many times with a simple picture break. The best thing to do is to apply Iron-on Vinyl to fake leather perfectly and it couldn't be easier!

You would need:

- Cricut maker or cutting machine

- Green Feather Iron on Vinyl

- EasyPress 2 thin

- Cricut Iron on Protective pad

- Cricut Design Space Instructions cactus

Directions

1. Place the iron on the side of the mat in color vinyl down to cut it.

2. Weed out excess plastic, cool 14 cactus.

3. I love the bright iron foil! Cut off all the cacti.

4.   Then inside the fake leather tote placed the EasyPress pad.

5.   Line the cactus to know the distance for the finished product you want. The first one or three is then mounted.

6.   The protective surface should be sealed.

7.   Set the EasyPress 2 to the proper false leather configuration. It can be slightly cooler at 295 to keep the tote from melting and squeezed at once for five seconds. Then another five seconds pulled.

8.   Tap on the EasyPress firmly.

9.   Repeat for every cacti cluster.

10.   Let the vinyl completely cool down and then remove plastic sheet from the container.

11.   Simple, when cooled down, to peel off. Re-press if necessary if it doesn't look like it is adhered to.

12.   Now the bag is ready to fill and remove from the city with all kinds of goodies. It's also a great homemade gift!

The Pen Holder Clasp Mini Leather Journal with Cricut Maker

First of all, for everyone on your list, you can make great gifts. My favorite are handmade gifts... but I want to ensure that they're of the highest standards. The manufacturer is incredible, because she can cut fabric, wood, leather, falsifying leather, chipboard etc.! Here's a great project I've developed, and I'm giving you free – Merry Christmas.

You would need:

- Cricut EasyPress 2 Small

- Cricut Iron-On Patent Protection

- Mini Composition Book

- Cricut Design Space

Directions:

1. Slide in the mat and place in the holder the marking wheel. The first result of the project will be.

2. Then remove a marker, and replace it with the fine blade. During this process do not remove the mat. Simply replace the blade and press C.

3. You can cut out the forms fast, and remove them from the mat.

4. Cut a few vinyl pictures out of iron. The pictures need only be 1.75 cm or less.

5. Heat up to 300* your EasyPress 2 and place the iron-on journal cover on the EasyPress mat.

6. Cover and press EasyPress 2 15 seconds. Cover with protection plate. This is it! This is it!

7. Let the iron-on refresh fully... the carrier sheet then flake back.

8. The time for cement rubber now.

9. Cut a faux leather scrap piece that covers the diary slits. Add the backside of the diary and the top side of the piece cut with rubber cement... do not put the slit on the piece.

10. Dry the cement rubber and cover the smaller piece with the slits.

11. Then put the cement on the top of the diary book and the cover of the inside of it. Tacky, let them dry.

12. Press the rubber cement book of the leather and then line up and press. Apply rubber cement to the back of the book and leather inside. No cement rubber between the lines scored. Allow the rubber cement to dry and then pick and press.

13. Press firmly down to secure your book. The book will remain perfect until you have a new book of fillers to peel and glue off. Leather can be used again in this way!

14. Please fold over the top flap and insert in a slit loop a mini pen or a regular pen. It makes the journal's perfect fastening! Never sit down without a pen for writing or sketching.

15. This project only takes 15 minutes when Cricut Maker is set up and ready to go. That's the best handmade donation or stocking cushion!

Leather Foil Iron-on Name Gift Tag Cricut Maker's Keychains!

The Cricut Maker is incredible... totally one step up from the awesome Explore Air 2. If you're in the machine market... get the Maker, or you'll want to do it every time. The Maker can do stuff no other machine could have done before. The Cricut Maker is a major investment but the amount it can make is limitless! It has extra pressure so that it can use knife blades, scores or rotary blades, all of which are major game changers. Each day of the week, I use my Cricut. Make gifts, save time, make everything. The Cricut Maker has so many more options and thus much more ways (if it is your business). If you're a newbie, the Maker Spring—or you'll always want to. You start with Paper and Vinyl and then move quickly to iron-on and more. The learning curve is fast. You're going to want to cut textile, board, chipboard, leather in no time... you want to scoring paper and cut patterns in fabric. Get the Cricut Maker so that you have space to develop.

Let me show you how easy it is to make these honeymoon keys... perfect for gift tags that can be used in zip pulls, keychains, baggage tags, etc.

You will need:

- Cricut Iron-on Foil in rose gold

- Cricut EasyPress 2 Small

- Cricut EasyPress Mat

- Cricut Tools

- Cricut True Control Knife

- Cricut Self-Healing Mat

- Keychain Lanyards

- Cricut Normal and Strong Grip Cutting

- Cricut Self-Healing

- Cricut EasyPress 2 Small

- Criciut EasyPress

Directions:

1. Start by opening up Cricut Design Space

2. Design Space comes complete with many font, pictures and characteristics so that it can be used immediately after you plug into it. You can easily upload your own images, but the project today will only use a Cricut fountain.

3. Create and open a textbox to a new canvas. Specify your name, and in the drop-down list, select the ZOO DAY

font. The all-cap fonts are perfect for this. It works great. When the name has been written down, the letter space is decreased so that the letters start to touch each other. Touch them before and after each letter.

4.   You can check out my project here, but your own custom names must be created.

5.   Make it visible to both layers.

6.   Changing the iron-on vinyl color from the top layer to the color... or closing.

7.   Double every name now.

8.   The background of one version must be visible, the other the front.

9.   Select and solder every single name. All letters will be merged into one solid piece.

10.   After soldering, the background is solid and each name is solid. Choose and sweat or join all the blue names. Repeat the yellow names soldering.

11.   Click on the button to make it.

12.   On two separate mats you will bring up the sold or attached words.

13. Mirror the front-end mat picture. Then, with a glittering side, place the iron-on vinyl on your mat. Set the Iron-on Foil configuration of the machine.

14. Click on the "C" button and insert it into the Cricut Maker. It will cut the picture with the fine dot blade beautifully.

15. Remove the vinyl iron and trim the edges once cut. Set it above your Bright Pad Cricut and see where you should weed. It has a breeze. To remove excess vinyl, use the weeding tool.

16. Get the leather ready for the second mat. Leather cutting was never so easy with the Blade and the Builder Knife.

17. To help protect your cutting mat against leather, use the contact paper. Remove the leather packaging and turn it roughly onto it.

18. Place the paper and securely paste it on clear contact paper. Cut the leather in plastic.

19. Slide onto the machine and put the chrome blade in the machine to the right.

20. Make certain you have calibrated the blade beforehand.

21. Put the leather-covered contact paper right on the strong grip mat.

22. Place the blade in the Cricut Maker and have a chrome blade easily cut the leather.

Rose Gold Leather Earrings DIY

With a Cricut Maker you can do so many incredible things! Some honeymoon earrings only take a few minutes to make. The earrings of the leather are perfect because they can be very large, but they are lightweight and wear comfortable. These golden roses are great!

Make a fast pair of earrings for a gift, for wear and fun, and make a bunch for sale!

Supplies Required:

- Cricut Maker

- Cricut Strong Grip Mat

- Clear Contact Paper

- Cricut Metalic Rose Gold Vinyl

- Cricuts tools

- Hook and jump rings

- Criticut Metal leather Gold Cricut

Directions:

1. Start by stitching a clear contact paper to the back side of the leather. This keeps everything from the matt surface and keeps the mat more useful. Place the leather on the strong grip mat (contact paper side down).

2. To design a rope shape with a tiny hole cut at the top, use Cricut Design Space. Cut it off, then. I shouted I was using the blade for the knife, but I was too tired to switch to it.

3. And the leather wasn't really cut all around its rear edge, so there's a bit of fluff. I cut it off with the scissors of Cricut.

4. Then use some pins to attach a hook on the leather earring.

5. Cut some sweet shapes out of metallic rose vinyl gold. These are the forms in the Cricut Access file I found on a CDS.

6. Then peel the leather and stick it to the back. The rose-gold and rose-gold vinyl go hand in hand.

7. Under the layers of leather, I like the hit metallic.

8. Such a simple DIY for a good declaration pair of earrings.

Chapter 9 Other Cricut Project

How to Make Unicorn Wine Glass

Supplies Needed

- Stemless wine glasses

- Outdoor vinyl in the color of your choice

- Vinyl transfer tape

- Cutting mat

- Weeding tool or pick

- Extra fine glitter in the color of your choice

- Mod Podge

Directions:

1. Open Cricut Design Space and create a new project.

2. Select the "Text" button in the Design Panel.

3. Type "It's not drinking alone if my unicorn is here."

4. Using the dropdown box, select your favorite font.

5. Adjust the positioning of the letters, rotating some to give a whimsical look.

6. Select the "Image" button on the Design Panel and search for "unicorn."

7. Select your favorite unicorn and click "Insert," then arrange your design how you want it on the glass.

8. Place your vinyl on the cutting mat, making sure it is smooth and making full contact.

9. Send the design to your Cricut.

10. Use a weeding tool or pick to remove the excess vinyl from the design. Use the Cricut BrightPad to help if you have one.

11. Apply transfer tape to the design, pressing firmly and making sure there are no bubbles.

12. Remove the paper backing and apply the words to the glass where you'd like them. Leave at least a couple of inches at the bottom for the glitter.

13. Smooth down the design and carefully remove the transfer tape.

14. Coat the bottom of the glass in Mod Podge, wherever you would like glitter to be. Give the area a wavy edge.

15. Sprinkle glitter over the Mod Podge, working quickly before it dries.

16. Add another layer of Mod Podge and glitter, and set it aside to dry.

17. Cover the glitter in a thick coat of Mod Podge.

18. Allow the glass to cure for at least 48 hours.

19. Enjoy drinking from your unicorn wine glass!

How to Make Clutch Purse?

Supplies Needed

- Two fabrics, one for the exterior and one for the interior

- Fusible fleece

- Fabric cutting mat

- D-ring

- Sew-on snap

- Lace

- Zipper

- Sewing machine

- Fabric scissors

- Keychain or charm of your choice Instructions

Directions:

1. Open Cricut Design Space and create a new project.

2. Select the "Image" button in the lower left-hand corner and search for "essential wallet."

3. Select the essential wallet template and click "Insert."

4. Place the fabric on the mat.

5. Send the design to the Cricut.

6. Remove the fabric from the mat.

7. Attach the fusible fleecing to the wrong side of the exterior fabric.

8. Attach lace to the edges of the exterior fabric.

9. Assemble the D-ring strap.

10. Place the D-ring onto the strap and sew into place.

11. Fold the pocket pieces wrong side out over the top of the zipper, and sew it into place.

12. Fold the pocket's wrong side in and sew the sides.

13. Sew the snap onto the pocket.

14. Lay the pocket on the right side of the main fabric lining so that the corners of the pocket's bottom are behind the curved edges of the lining fabric. Sew the lining piece to the zipper tape.

15. Fold the lining behind the pocket and iron in place.

16. Sew on the other side of the snap.

17. Trim the zipper so that it's not overhanging the edge.

18. Sew the two pocket layers to the exterior fabric across the bottom.

19. Sew around all of the layers.

20. Trim the edges with fabric scissors.

21. Turn the clutch almost completely inside out and sew the opening closed.

22. Turn the clutch all the way inside out and press the corners into place.

23. Attach your charm or keychain to the zipper.

24. Carry your new clutch wherever you need it!

How to Make Buntings and Other Party Decoration with Cricut Machine

Supplies needed for bunting:

- Fabric

- Fabric stabilizer

- Ribbon

- Iron-on glitter vinyl

- Fabric adhesive

- Inkjet printer

- Cricut machine

- Weeding tool

- Transfer Tape

- Needle

- Thread

- Fancy multicolored buttons

- Iron

- Grease-proof paper

Directions:

1. Log in to the Cricut design space.

2. Click on Create a New Project.

3. Use the Insert Shape icon to select the basic shape you want the bunting to be in. (I will explain using the star shape.)

4. Highlight and unlock the Padlock at the lower side of the shape.

5. Edit or resize the shape to your content.

6. Copy and paste the shape as much as required by your text.

7. Click on the Text icon.

8. Type in your text: "Happy Birthday."

9. Choose the font that you want the text cut in.

10. Move to the preview screen.

11. Adjust the shapes to the size of your fabric.

12. Apply the fabric to the cutting mat.

13. Push the cutting mat up against the rollers.

14. Load the mat into the machine.

15. Set the cutting dial to custom.

16. Select the fabric setting.

17. Click Go.

18. Cut out your shapes on the fabric.

19. Cut out the shapes on the fabric stabilizer too.

20. Place the iron-on glitter vinyl shiny side down on the cutting mat.

21. Load the mat into the machine.

22. Push the cutting mat against the rollers.

23. Set the dial to iron-on glitter vinyl setting.

24. Cut out your text with the Cricut machine.

25. Unload the mat.

26. Remove the iron-on vinyl.

27. Use the weeding tool to weed out the waste from the vinyl.

28. Apply transfer tape to your vinyl.

29. Cut each letter of the text separately.

30. Glue the fabric shape together with the fabric stabilizer.

31. Ensure there is no air bubble and that the edges do not overlap.

32. Turn down a point of the buntings to make it "hangable."

33. Sew a button each to the turned-down edge of the buntings.

34. Prepress the bunting shape with a medium-heat iron for some seconds.

35. Apply each vinyl letter on each bunting.

36. Place a grease-proof paper on it.

37. Apply a medium-heat iron on it for thirty seconds.

38. Peel away the transfer tape.

39. Reapply the paper and press again with medium heat iron for few seconds.

40. Tie a bow with the ribbon at one end.

41. Thread the ribbon through the turned-down part of the buntings until all the buntings are linked together by the ribbon.

42. Tie the other end of the ribbon to keep the buntings in place.

43. Your buntings are ready to be hanged.

44. To make any other type of buntings requires this same process; the only difference would be the text and shape.

How to Make Christmas Ornament with Cricut machine

Supplies needed are as follows:

- Cricut machine

- Cricut glitter vinyl

- Transfer tape

- Scraper tool

- Weeding tool

- Ribbon

Directions:

1. Log in to the Cricut design space and start a new project.

2. Click on the Input icon.

3. Type in your Christmas greetings.

4. Change the text font.

5. Ungroup and adjust the spacing.

6. Highlight and "weld" to design the overlapping letters.

7. Select the parts of the text you do not want as part of the final cut.

8. Readjust the text size.

9. Select the file as a cut file. You will get to preview the design as a cut file.

10. Approve the cut file.

11. The text is ready to cut.

12. Place the vinyl on the cutting mat shiny side down.

13. Load the mat into the machine.

14. Custom dial to vinyl.

15. Cut the image.

16. Use the weeding tool to remove excess vinyl after the image is cut.

17. Apply a layer of transfer tape to the top of the cut vinyl.

18. Peel back the vinyl paperback.

19. Apply the vinyl onto the glass ornament.

20. Go over the applied vinyl with a scraper tool to remove air bubble underneath the vinyl.

21. Slowly peel away the transfer tape from the glass ornament.

How to Make Tassels

Supplies Needed

- 12" x 18" fabric rectangles

- Fabric mat

- Glue gun

Directions:

1. Open Cricut Design Space and create a new project.

2. Select the "Image" button in the lower left-hand corner and search "tassel."

3. Select the image of a rectangle with lines on each side and click "Insert."

4. Place the fabric on the cutting mat.

5. Send the design to the Cricut.

6. Remove the fabric from the mat, saving the extra square.

7. Place the fabric face down and begin rolling tightly, starting on the uncut side. Untangle the fringe as needed.

8. Use some of the scrap fabric and a hot glue gun to secure the tassel at the top.

9. Decorate whatever you want with your new tassels!

How to Make Monogrammed Drawstring Bag

Supplies Needed

• Two matching rectangles of fabric

• Needle and thread

• Ribbon

• Heat transfer vinyl

• Cricut EasyPress or iron

• Cutting mat

- Weeding tool or pick

Directions:

1. Open Cricut Design Space and create a new project.

2. Select the "Image" button in the lower left-hand corner and search "monogram."

3. Select the monogram of your choice and click "Insert."

4. Place the iron-on material shiny liner side down on the cutting mat.

5. Send the design to the Cricut.

6. Use the weeding tool or pick to remove excess material.

7. Remove the monogram from the mat.

8. Center the monogram on your fabric, then move it a couple of inches down so that it won't be folded up when the ribbon is drawn.

9. Iron the design onto the fabric.

10. Place the two rectangles together, with the outer side of the fabric facing inward.

11. Sew around the edges, leaving a seam allowance. Leave the top open and stop a couple of inches down from the top.

12. Fold the top of the bag down until you reach your stitches.

13. Sew along the bottom of the folded edge, leaving the sides open.

14. Turn the bag right side out.

15. Thread the ribbon through the loop around the top of the bag.

16. Use your new drawstring bag to carry what you need!

How to Make Paw Print Socks

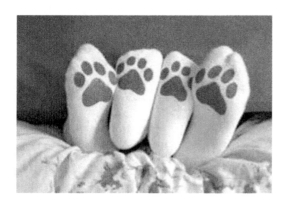

Supplies Needed

- Socks

- Heat transfer vinyl

- Cutting mat

- Scrap cardboard

- Weeding tool or pick

- Cricut EasyPress or iron

Directions:

1. Open Cricut Design Space and create a new project.

2. Select the "Image" button in the lower left-hand corner and search "paw prints."

3. Select the paw prints of your choice and click "Insert."

4. Place the iron-on material on the mat.

5. Send the design to the Cricut.

6. Use the weeding tool or pick to remove excess material.

7. Remove the material from the mat.

8. Fit the scrap cardboard inside of the socks.

9. Place the iron-on material on the bottom of the socks.

10. Use the EasyPress to adhere it to the iron-on material.

11. After cooling, remove the cardboard from the socks.

12. Wear your cute paw print socks!

Chapter 10 Tips and Tricks to make Cricut machine easier and efficient

The Cricut Maker and Explore Air 2 are great machines that can be used to do a lot of things. However, new and first time owners find it a little challenging to get their heads over the machines, thus, making it difficult for them to utilize the machines to their full potentials.

For crafters that get little or no support from experienced users, it takes quite some time for them to really get a hold of the machines and finally maximize their output.

If you've purchased or intend to purchase a Cricut machine, then you must know that there are tips and tricks you can apply to boost the machine's output and ensure optimum functionality.

Most of the tips are geared towards helping beginners understand their Cricut machines; however, there are also other advanced tips for veterans. Below are some of the tips and tricks;

Make sure you subscribe to Cricut Access

If you own a Cricut Explore Air 2, you have to subscribe to Cricut Access in order to get the best out of it. There are two subscription plans – the yearly plan and the monthly plan.

Having an active subscription plan with Cricut Access will save you a lot of money because you won't have to buy individual projects and images. With Cricut Access, you'll have access to over 375 fonts, thousands of projects and over 370 fonts. Plus, it's less stressful to pay a flat than to always worry about the amount of money you'll be spending on projects.

Always de-tact your Cutting Mat

The Cricut Maker comes with the blue light grip mat, while the Explore Air 2 normally comes with the green standard cutting mat. Before putting on the machine, make sure you always place your materials onto the mat first.

Even with the right tools, it can be very difficult to get off the cardstock when it's new, and this results in damaged projects sometimes. The blue light grip mat doesn't have such problems, thus, instead of de-tacking the green mat, you can purchase it for your card and paper projects.

Make sure you keep your Cutting Mat Covers

New cutting mats always come with a plastic shield that covers them, and they are easily pulled off and on. Whatever you do, make sure you don't misplace the cover, and always put it back on the mat whenever you're done using it – this practice helps to keep the mat sticky and clean for over longer periods.

Make sure you clean the Cutting Mat

Whenever you use your cutting mat, make sure you clean it afterward, and it is recommended that you use nonalcoholic baby wipes. If you do this consistently, it'll reduce the buildup of vinyl and cardstock residue, as well as dust stains and other regular lint that float about.

Make sure you acquire the right tools

To fully maximize the Cricut machine experience, you have acquired the Cricut Tool Set. The set contains a scraper, a weeding tool, scissors, and a spatula. If your craft involves cutting either heat transfer vinyl or adhesive vinyl, then the weeding tool is a Must. The other tools come in handy for different activities and projects.

Purchase the Scoring Stylus

The scoring stylus is mandatory for a whole lot of card projects. Thus, without it, your options will be limited, and it doesn't come with the machine at purchase. However, if you buy your machine as part of a bundle, there's a high probability that I'll be included, so you need to check.

Your first project should be your sample project

As a beginner, who just bought the Cricut machine, your first project should be the sample project. When you purchase the Explore Air 2, you'll realize that the machine is loaded with sample cardstock for users to make their first cards. The supporting materials are minimal and it is just one card. Thus, instead of embarking on a huge and fancy project, you can embark on a simple project so that you can get a feel of how things work – hardware and software wise.

Test Cuts

Before you carry out any serious project, make sure to do a test cut first, because there are a number of things that can possibly go wrong. For example, if you set the blade too high, it might not cut the cardstock or vinyl properly. Also, if you set the blade too low, it could possibly ruin the cutting mat.

Make sure you always replace pen lids after use

A lot of crafters have the habit of forgetting their pen inside the machine when they're done with their projects. It can happen to anyone, but to make sure the pen ink doesn't dry out, it is important to get the lid on it as soon as you're done with your project. Cricut pen is very expensive, and maybe that's the reason why Design Space always prompts users to get their lids back on.

You should link your old cartridges to your Design Space Account

If you have any Cricut cartridge(s) from an old Cricut machine, you can link it up to your new account. The procedure is fast and simple; however, you have to understand that each cartridge can only be linked once. Thus, if you intend to buy a used cartridge, you have to confirm that it hasn't been linked to another account already.

Getting Materials off the Cutting Mat

Rather than using conventional tools for removing vinyl or cardstock from the cutting mat, you can consider another method. When people peel their projects from the mat, it can possibly result in curling, thus, you should peel the mat away from the project instead. In addition, you should also do the unconventional method of bending the mat away from the card.

When you do this, the mat might turn upside down and bend one corner to life the cardstock. At this stage, you can just place the spatula under to take off your project. Some people use their credit cards to take off the mat, and as much as this might work, it can also damage the adhesive on the mat.

Purchase the Deep Cut Blade

One of the most painful things in the world of crafting is embarking on a project without the right tools. Unlike the Maker, you need to have the Deep Cut Blade for the Explore Air 2 to be able to cut through thicker leather, card, chipboard, and others. When you order the blade, you should also order the blade housing too. Furthermore, you don't have to wait till you need it urgently before you order for it. Buy it today.

Use free SVG files in order to cut the cost

In terms of designing projects, you don't have to be fully dependent on Design Space store. You have other options; there's the option of creating your personal SVG files or using some other free SVG files on the internet. There are a number of websites on the internet that have so many free SVG files. All you have to do in order to locate them is to carry out minimal research on the internet.

Make sure you Load the mat properly

Before you start cutting, you must be sure that your mat is loaded properly. It must be placed under the rollers. If the mat is not loaded properly, the machine may not cut at all, or in other cases, it might start cutting before the top of the grip on the mat.

Different pens work in the Explore Air 2

The Cricut pens are not the only ones that work in the Explore Air 2 machine. Examples of other pens that can work with the machine include but not limited to, American Craft Pens and Sharpie Pens. With that said, you should have it at the back of your mind that Cricut pens are of the highest quality and are known to last longer than others.

Make use of free front for some of your projects

On the internet, there are a number of websites where you can get free fonts to use for your designs. To do this, you need to visit the sites and download the fonts, install them to your system and load on your Cricut Design Space.

Installation of Fonts into Design Space

When you install the fonts, the next step is to load them into Design Space. Thus, in order to achieve this, you have to sign out of Design Space and re-sign in. After that, you'll also have to restart your PC. When this is done, you can check your Design Space account, where you'll see the new fonts in the display.

Changing/replacing blades

Just like everything in life, nothing lasts forever, and Cricut blades are known to wear out. You will know it's time to change the blade when the cuts are no longer effective and smooth. That is the most obvious sign, however, there are a couple of others including; tearing vinyl or card, lifting of vinyl off the backing sheet, and halfway cuts (wrong cut settings can also be responsible for this). If you're convinced that your blades are no longer effective, you have to purchase new ones.

When the mat is no longer sticky

The most proactive way of keeping your mat healthy over a long period is by cleaning it. However, if the mat is beyond redemption and there is no replacement yet, you should tape down your vinyl or card for it to stick. While tapping, you shouldn't tape the areas that are meant to be cut, just tape the sides. Most people use the medium tack painter tape because it allows a lot of room for this type of action, and it does not damage the cardstock.

Custom settings for Cricut machines

There are 7 preset options on the dial for Explore Air 2, and they include;

1. Cardstock

2. Paper

3. Iron-on

4. Vinyl

5. Posterboard

6. Light cardstock

7. Bonded fabric

There is a custom option for materials that are not included in the cutting list, and you select it on the dial.

To do this, open Design Space, choose your project and press 'Make it." At this point, you'll see a prompt with a drop-down menu, where you'll be able to choose your material.

Likewise, you can also create a new custom material. There are resources on the Cricut website and all other the internet, regarding the creation of custom material.

Chapter 11.   Cricut Project

Coffee Mugs

Arranging gifts for your family, extended family, friends, and relatives can get overwhelming sometimes. But not anymore! Since everyone is a coffee, tea, or hot chocolate lover, so why gift mugs in this holiday season. Read on to know how to make an inexpensive Christmas coffee mugs at home in 10 minutes.

Here's what you will need: Cricut Explore Air 2, Cricut Design Space, black vinyl or silver vinyl, clear transfer tape or paper, coffee mug, "I just want to drink hot cocoa and watch Christmas movies" cut file or "hot chocolate is like a hug from inside" cut file

1. Open Cricut Design Space, begin a new project, and then use Cricut Design Space Image Library to select any image you want to work with. Or you can design the saying in any photo editing program like Adobe Illustrator. For example, in this project, I uploaded the design of saying, "I just want to drink hot cocoa and watch Christmas movies." Another example is the saying, "hot chocolate is like a hug."

2. Make sure to adjust the color or material of the design as you like. I use black vinyl for the lettering of "I just want to drink hot cocoa and watch Christmas movies," and silver and silver and red vinyl for the lettering of "I just want to drink hot cocoa and watch Christmas movies." And, then upload I uploaded the design into Cricut Design. Make sure to keep the size of the mug in mind before designing the sayings.

3. Set the Cricut machine for cutting by setting the dial as per the material you are cutting.

4. When done, cut the vinyl to remove excess vinyl letting from the design by using a Cricut Weeder Tool.

5. You can now apply the vinyl stencil to a mug of your choice by using transfe

6. r tape and remove air bubbles by using a smoothing tool.

3D Paper Flowers

Paper flowers are a beautiful way to decorate a gift. Creating paper flowers through the Cricut machine is very easy. Make one flower for a gift or convert it into a bouquet for a larger gift; it's up to you.

The flower for this project is a rolled flower, but you can easily customize the design in Cricut Design Space and mix and match flowers to create flowers of all kinds.

Here's what you will need: Cricut Explore Air 2, Cricut Design Space, Cricut quilling tool, Cardstock, Cricut StandardGrip mat, and glue.

1. Select the image and for this, open Cricut Design space and find the images for flowers in the Flower Shoppe cartridge or simply click on the following link

https://design.cricut.com/#/design/new/images/cartridge/288.
Scroll the images, select the style of the flower you like, click on insert image, and place it on your canvas. You have ten options for spirals and 40 options for flowers and leaves. Resize the spirals, flowers, and leaves to fit your project.

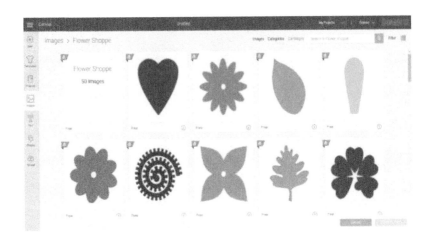

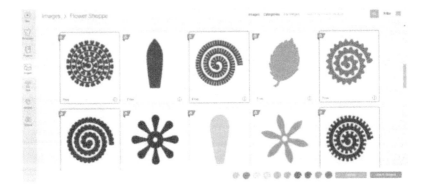

2. Place cardstock onto the cutting mat, then load it into the Cricut machine, set the dial to that material, and press the cut/go button on the machine to cut spirals.

3. When done, cut out the flower spirals and gently remove them from the mat.

4. Quill the flowers and for this, take the quilling tool, place the end of flower spiral in its slot and then start turning it clockwise to roll spiral. Hold the spiral by placing your index finger under the spiral roll so that the layers aren't disturbed.

5. Place a drop of glue on the circle in the middle of spiral, place the rolled flower on it, let it open slightly, and press flower for a minute or two until the glue holds it.

And now you have your very own paper flower.

Feel free to customize them according to your requirements. The following are great options.

Leather Pillow

Leather pillows are great for your holiday décor this year. They will match well with your Christmas tree and other holiday throw pillows. Here's how you can create one by using the Cricut machine.

Here's what you will need: Cricut Explore Air 2, Cricut Design Space, standard cutting mat, ¾ yard of pillow cover in linen-look fabric, white or red, ¼ yard of faux leather, Cricut weeder tool, pillow insert, black heat transfer vinyl, sewing machine with leather sewing needle, thread, iron, fabric shears, heat and bond ultra

1. Open Cricut Design space and create a Christmas tree pattern in the canvas.

   You can also upload the Christmas tree and then arrange them in a design on the canvas that would fit your pillow cover.

2. Now it's time for cutting. If your pillow is large, you may have to cut trees in the section, so first decide which of the Christmas trees would be cut from the leather and delete the rest of the trees.

3. Place a heat transfer vinyl onto the cutting mat, then load it into the Cricut machine, set the dial to Faux leather material, and press the cut/go button on the machine to cut trees.

4. When done, cut out the vinyl Christmas trees and then cut a tree from cardstock to use it as a stencil to cut out leather trees by using fabric shears.

Vinyl trees and leather trees

5. You can now permanently attached Christmas trees with the help of fabric glue or have them stitch into the pillow cover with matching thread. Make sure your sewing machine is stitching by using a leather sewing needle for this.

6. When done, insert a pillow into the cover and place them as you wanted.

Leather Key Ring

Another inexpensive holiday gift is a leather key fob. And the best part, key fobs can be personalized in any way by using Cricut pens. Make a bunch of these rings and give them as gifts and use one for yourself.

Here's what you will need: Cricut Explore Air 2, Cricut Design Space, standard cutting mat, faux leather in brown or blue, Circut pen in black for personalization, Gorilla glue, keyrings, rivet, paper crafting set, key fob templates

1. Open Cricut Design Space and then open templates for key fobs. You can even use your design and play with them in Design Space.

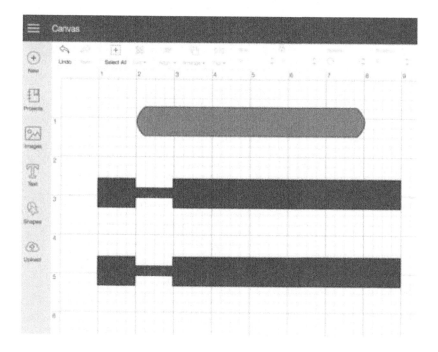

2. Select the designs for key fobs, then load the Cricut machine, set the dial to that Faux leather material, and press the cut/go button on the machine. Insert Cricut pen if you want your designs to be personalized.

3. Use a piercer to poke to fit the rivet, and then slide the keyring onto the key fob. Push the longer end of the rivet through the back of fob, place the rivet mallet on top and then strike it with a handle of a hammer to set it.

4. And that's it. Here's how your key fob will look.

Here's a challenge for you

Conclusion

Cricut may seem complicated at first, but there is a lot you can do with this machine – and a lot that you can get out of it. If you feel confused by Cricut, then take your time, get familiar with the buttons, and start having fun with it.

With Cricut, anything is possible. If you've been wondering what you can do with your machine, the simple answer is almost anything. For designers, for those who like to make precise cuts, and for those who like to print their own shirts, this is a wonderful option to consider. If you are thinking of getting a Cricut machine, you'll see here that there is a lot that you can do with this unique tool, and endless creative possibilities.

The next step is simple – if you have a Cricut machine, get familiar with it. Learn more about it and see for yourself some of the fun things you can do with Cricut, and the cool basic projects you can try now.

If you have a Cricut machine and you've not gotten these supplies I would advise that you get them as soon as possible. We are aware that these supplies are grouped into different categories. First is the paper category which includes; adhesive cardstock, cereal box, copy paper, flocked paper, cardboard paper, Notebook paper, flocked cardstock, foil embossed paper, Freezer Paper, Glitter Paper, Kraft paper, Kraft Board, metallic Paper, Metallic Poster board, Photographs, Photo Framing Mat, Poster Board, Rice Paper, Wax Paper, Solid core Cardstock, White Core Cardstock, Photo Framing mat, Watercolor Paper, Freezer Paper, Foil Poster Board, etc.

It can help you make a lot of handmade things which not only save you money but your time as well blessing you with beautiful products that you can use for yourself as well as the gift to others. You can make handmade cards, design your t-shirt, create your ornaments, and design an envelope and many more.

If you have yet to purchase your first machine, I hope this helps your decision. We want you to enjoy Cricut projecct ideas and much as thousands of users around the world. Keep the tips and tricks provided close by as a reference guide so you aren't searching all over to find the answers to your questions.

Never stop doing research. Never stop trying new things. Never, ever stop being creative. The Cricut does not make you any less creative; it just makes the process easier so that you can focus your valuable time and efforts on more important things or personalizing the projects after making the cuts. It takes the tedious work out of your hands and makes everything fun, easy, and fast.